The
Great
Leeds
Pub
Crawl

First published in Great Britain in 2011 by The Derby Books Publishing Company Limited, Derby, DE21 4SZ.

Paperback mono edition published in Great Britain in 2012 by The Derby Books Publishing Company Limited, 3 The Parker Centre, Derby, DE21 4SZ.

ISBN 978-1-78091-234-9

Printed and bound by Copytech (UK) Limited, Peterborough.

The
Great
Leeds
Pub
Crawl

Simon Jenkins

Contents

Acknowledgements

For their encouragement I owe a debt of gratitude to the great and good of British beer writing, many of whom I am privileged to count as friends, including Roger Protz, Zak Avery, Barrie Pepper, Alastair Gilmour, Pete Brown and Adrian Tierney-Jones; to Steve Brooke and Nigel McDermid who got me started on the rocky road of beer writing and to the late Michael Jackson who proved a critical friend early in my career.

Equally, I am grateful to those who have joined me on the various expeditions needed to assemble this guide, and who suffered in silence as I wrote my scratchy little notes – my wife Katrina and our children Ben and Hannah and my great mates Martin Edwards, Tamsin Wragg and Gareth Dunworth. For their help and support along the way I would like to thank Paul Napier of the *Yorkshire Evening Post* and my university colleagues Rachel Casey and Rebecca Messenger-Clark.

Thanks to Ian Moss at Budweiser Budvar, Sam Moss at Leeds Brewery and Jake's Bar for providing prizes for the competition, to Sharon Brigden at SLBPR for her help and support with photographs and information, to Greg Mulholland MP for his Otley Pub Crawl suggestions – and to photographer Mark Bickerdike for riding to my assistance with his Nikon at the 11th hour.

Thanks also to Denis Cox of Budweiser Budvar, who has been telling me for years that I should write a book. It's not *The Good Soldier Sjvek*, Denis, but I hope you like it anyhow.

Introduction

The public house is a uniquely British institution, quite distinct in character and tradition from its equivalent overseas. Equally special is crafted British real ale – whether it has been produced by the same family concern for centuries or created amid the concrete and gleaming steel of a new-build brewery on a soulless industrial estate.

Our better pubs have also introduced us to the fabulous world of beer from beyond these shores – lovely craft beers from America, wheat beers from Germany, traditional lagers from the Czech Republic, and the jaw-dropping range of styles and flavours which have been created over many centuries in Belgium.

Through the brewers' art, through their delicate, nuanced use of different yeast strains and varieties of hop and malt, the beers produced can vary massively in strength, texture and colour, while offering a whole range of flavours from sharp and citric to chocolatey, treacly and burnt, from sweet to sour, by way of biscuit, passion fruit, nuts, earthiness, whisky – and a whole lot more besides.

There is more variety out there, both in premises and product, to inject the simple act of going to the pub with the endless capacity to delight and surprise.

The 35 pubs and bars on my Great Leeds Pub Crawl are some of my personal favourites and between them represent a broad cross-section of the licensed premises to be found in my home town.

Aside from these 35, I have suggested many others around the city which are also worthy of your custom. Even so, it is not a comprehensive list, and is largely limited to the area bounded by the Leeds Outer Ring Road, and doubtless some readers will feel aggrieved that their own personal favourite did not make it into print.

The ones which did each have something special to justify their inclusion, while my suggestion of some detours and some alternative pub crawls in Chapel Allerton, Otley, around Leeds University campus, along Great George Street – plus the infamous Otley Run – should hopefully satisfy everyone.

Simon Jenkins
25 July 2011

www.greatleedspubcrawl.blogspot.com

Pub Crawl One

The Heritage Route

This is comfortably the longest walk described in this book, and its distance could be cut in half by simply ignoring the first pub and starting the trail at the Adelphi. Yet to do so would be to ignore the city's finest pub and its licensed premises most deserving of heritage status.

So, visit the Garden Gate, and if you can't face the long hike along cheerless Hunslet Road, get a taxi before completing this little jaunt through some of the city's most unspoiled and historic pubs. It takes in three obvious 19th-century choices – the Adelphi, Whitelock's and the Vic – though the others each have genuine historic merit of their own.

Directions:

The **Garden Gate** is in Whitfield Place at Hunslet but from here, a short dog-leg is required to get you to Low Road and Hunslet Road for the long route march into town. Follow this until you pass the Tetley Brewery site, turning right into Meadow Lane, and reaching the **Adelphi** after another 200 metres. Turn right out of here, cross Leeds Bridge and continue into Briggate. Turk's Head Yard and **Whitelock's** is on your left, about 100 metres north of Boar Lane; another 150 metres further north is Ship Yard – and The **Ship**. On leaving here, continue north before turning right into the Headrow and then left into Vicar Lane, reaching the **Templar** after about 150 metres on your right. From here it's almost due west along Merrion Street, passing the Merrion Centre, and then straight on into Great George Street to reach the **Victoria** on your right, just behind the Town Hall. From here, go back 50 metres, turning left into Calverley Street, passing Millennium Square to turn right into Portland Way beside the Civic Hall, and left into Woodhouse Lane, to reach the **Fenton** after about 200 metres, on your left.

Approximate total distance: 3.2 miles

Detours:

If you wish to add further venues to your walk, then visits to the **Mulberry** on Hunslet Road, the **Viaduct** on Lower Briggate and the **Pack Horse** on Briggate, can each be accommodated without seriously deviating from your route. Short detours after the Ship and the Victoria would bring you to the **Horse and Trumpet** on the Headrow and the **George** on Great George Street. And though the 21st-century **Cuthbert Brodrick** on Millennium Square hardly fits with the heritage theme of this pub crawl, its name does at least reference the architect of the Town Hall, Corn Exchange and Mechanics Institute – now Leeds City Museum – who did more than anyone to set the tone and character of Victorian Leeds.

The Garden Gate

Whitfield Place, Hunslet, LS10 2QB
0113 277 7708
www.gardengateleeds.co.uk

Our journey starts a mile out of town, where, in an unfashionable suburb and surrounded by low-rise offices and seventies housing, lies Leeds's most beautiful pub.

If the Garden Gate were in Briggate, or in a fashionable suburb – or close enough to the city centre to be part of the regular crawl – it would be lauded like Whitelock's and the Adelphi and prized yet more highly. Tourists would flock to this working museum and try a pint of traditional hand-pulled mild, Nikons clicking like grasshoppers.

But the Garden Gate hangs at the end of a characterless cul-de-sac in downtown Hunslet, lost in its surroundings. It has served this community since before Queen Victoria's reign. Abandoned changing rooms in the cellar speak of a time when it doubled as home to a local rugby side. The showers, the communal bath, the masseur's table, are all still there, relics of this glorious past.

Even so, it took a last-ditch campaign to save the Garden Gate from sacreligious destruction by the concrete-crazy planners of the seventies. And though it has endured some ups and downs since then, its future is now secure as part of the expanding Leeds Brewery empire. Where were once just illuminated beer fonts are now handpulls dispensing Leeds Best, Leeds Pale and Midnight Bell – the wonderful trinity of real ales which have gained such a hold on the affections of the city's drinkers these past few years.

It is a ceramic palace, from the ornate brown and cream tiled exterior, to the greens of the pub's long central corridor which divides little snugs, nooks and crannies from the two main drinking areas either side of a central bar.

The corridor is itself a gem, tiled from floor to ceiling, save for polished mahogany panels and panes of etched and decorated glass. The floor is an ornate tiled mosaic; a tiled archway arcs over the corridor. Wood, mirrors and glass predominate in each room, though it's the ceramic which makes this place truly special. No-one seems to know for sure, but it's only a part-romantic notion that these tiles were Burmantofts Faience, a relic of the time when the east Leeds suburb was famed for its pottery. The present building – a perfect example of late Victorian and early Edwardian architecture – dates from 1902, when pottery production at Burmantofts was still in full swing.

The curving bar counter, tiled floors and mahogany back bar of the Garden Gate's front room, the Vaults, is an absolute treasure, and alone worth the pub's recent elevation to Grade II* listed status.

Pub Architecture

Between the mahogany panelling of the **Adelphi**, the ceramic of the **Garden Gate** and the exuberant gaudy mirrors, stained glass, dark wood, brass and copper bar-top of **Whitelock's**, Leeds boasts some true gems of pub internal architecture. Others have merit: the curious mock Tudor of the **Templar**, the inter-war cosiness of the **Grove**, the Victorian utility of the **Cardigan Arms**.

Given the constant throughput of customers and regular changes of ownership and direction they have endured, it is remarkable that they have survived intact – though of course many others have been stripped of their character in the name of progress.

Like at the Garden Gate there are some further gems to be found in the suburbs, like the **Beech**, a thirties period piece in Wortley. The cosy **Albion** in Armley, famous as the model used for a 00-scale trackside pub in the old Hornby Railway, was sadly closed as we went to press.

Adelphi

Hunslet Road, Leeds Bridge, LS10 1JQ
0113 245 6377
www.theadelphileeds.co.uk

Just a few yards from the Tetley gates, the beautiful Adelphi was essentially the brewery tap for more than 100 years – the place where the staff would slake their thirst after long days in the brewhouse, in the bottling plant, the warehouses and the delivery vans.

Its frontage is a shapely, stately, elegant curve; stepping inside is to get a glimpse of just how much workmanship went into creating a Victorian city tavern.

Like the Garden Gate, Whitelock's and the Victoria – all stopping points on this first pub crawl – the Adelphi is a true pub gem, with its heavy doors framed with extravagant carved wooden surrounds, windows of floral etched glass, acres of lacquered wood and red tiles. Some of the seating is still separated by wood and glass screens which act as an effective baffle to conversation, while the pub's four separate high-ceilinged rooms each has its own character and ambience.

The bar, which stretches along the pub's central corridor fronts onto just one of these rooms and is topped with an interesting range of ales and a cosmopolitan choice of lagers, though Tetley's and fellow Yorkshire favourite Timothy Taylor Landlord remain very much the stock-in trade here.

With its days as the Tetley brewery tap now over, the Adelphi has re-invented itself as a gastropub – surprising alternatives like oyster and chestnut mushroom risotto or chicken and chorizo skewer with cassoulet and panzanella augment some more familiar pub dining choices.

Tetley Brewery

The walk from The Garden Gate to the Adelphi takes about 20 minutes and brings you directly past the sprawling Tetley brewery site, which was finally closed in June 2011.

Its bright red letters have shone through clouds of billowing steam for generations, as sure a 'Welcome to Leeds' for travellers arriving from the south as the ivory white of the Parkinson Tower, the stone grandeur of the Town Hall or the bronze bulk of the Black Prince. The beer itself was as much a part of the city as Roundhay Park, the City Varieties, Leeds United.

And you can still buy it, of course, though owners Carlsberg may have underestimated drinkers' passion for a local product, when they decided to switch production of the famous beer down south.

It marked the sad end of an era, which began when Joshua Tetley first leased the brewery in 1822. Over 150 years, its growth was rapid and at times almost exponential. Its output expanded to make it the world's largest producer of cask ale, and a chain of tied houses across Yorkshire made Tetley's and the famous hunstman logo utterly synonymous with Leeds.

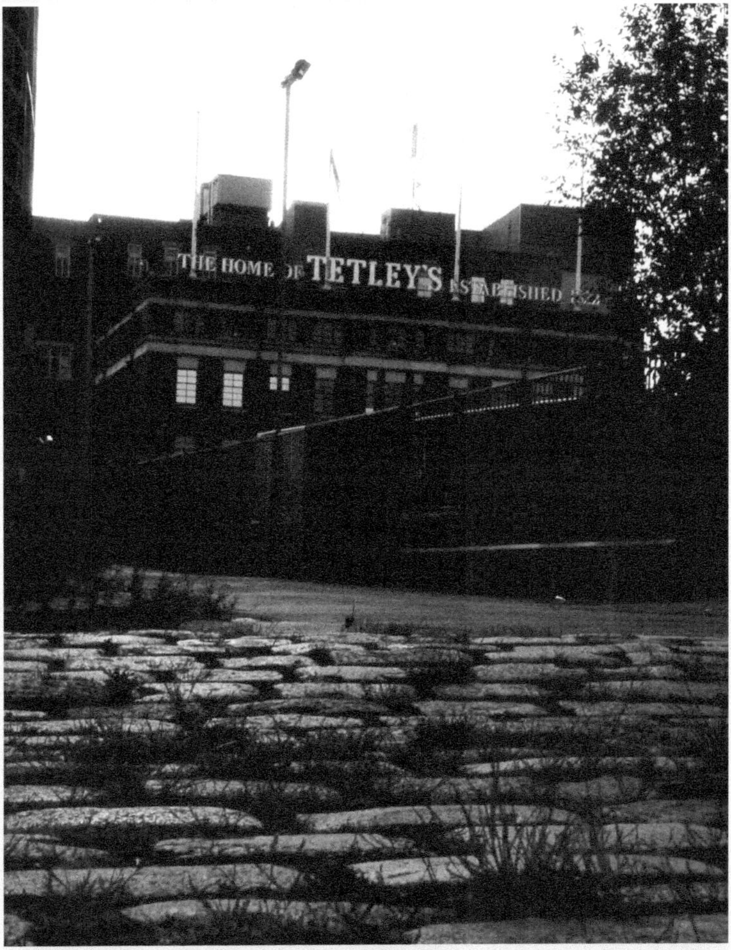
THE HOME OF TETLEY'S

TETLEY'S

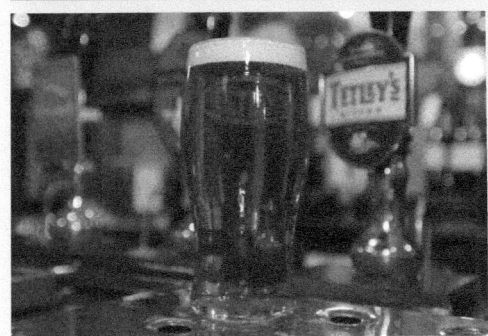

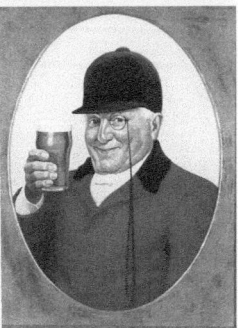

Whitelock's

Turk's Head Yard, Briggate, LS1 6HB
0113 245 3950

Leeds's most famous pub has endured a chequered recent history amid a sequence of bewildering changes of ownership, management and direction. Quality has suffered at times, and the availability of good real ales and decent food on offer has seemed crazily unpredictable, even from one week to the next. That it has survived relatively intact seems almost miraculous.

Yet, as the splendidly subtitled 'First City Luncheon Bar' it remains recognisably the same lively, welcoming hostelry which John Betjeman described as 'the very heart of Leeds', as much a home to shoppers, office staff, pensioners and loving couples as it is to visitors, wandering theatricals and passing poets.

Originally the Turk's Head, the pub was run by successive generations of the Whitelock family from the middle of the 19th century, until 1944, when it came under brewery ownership. The yard itself – a shortcut from Land's Lane to Briggate – retains this old name, which echoes with mystery, history and the resonance of past Crusades.

Despite being the city's best-known watering hole, Whitelock's has rarely served the city's most famous beer, if ever. For many years Scottish and Newcastle products dominated on the bar, and I don't think I have ever found Tetley's here. Leeds Brewery beers are now regulars on the counter, mind.

Amid the stained glass, polished brass and glinting mirrors, perhaps Whitelock's most remarkable feature is its beautiful curved bar front of sculptured tiles – the rich browns and creams, vibrant yellows and greens.

WHITELOCKS

Occupying a medieval Briggate burgage plot, it was first licensed as the Turk's Head in 1716. Rebuilt by the Whitelock family in the 1880s, it later extended into the row of Georgian working men's cottages. John Betjeman described it as 'the very heart of Leeds'

Its long outside yard is one of the city centre's great outdoor drinking spaces, and gives a clue to the 19th-century layout of the city. In 2006 Sarah Whitelock – a descendant of 1860s licensee John Lupton Whitelock – unveiled the pub's blue plaque for historical importance, the 100th to be awarded by Leeds Civic Trust.

Leeds's oldest pub

Whitelock's is routinely claimed to be the oldest pub in Leeds, though it isn't. By the time its first license was granted in 1715, trading had already been going on at the nearby Pack Horse for at least century.

The current Whitelock's was shaped by major alterations in 1886, though much of the exterior is likely to date back to 1784, when it was laid out as a pub, brewhouse and cottages. By contrast, when the Pack Horse was re-modelled in the 1980s all of its original character was lost.

Both, by the way, are relative striplings, compared to the Bingley Arms, a few miles east of the city at Bardsey, where detailed records show all the innkeepers and brewers over the ten centuries since Samson Elys was first documented as serving those travelling between Leeds and York in 953 AD.

The Bingley is one of a handful nationwide which claim to be Britain's oldest – a rivalry which even the *Guinness Book of Records* has failed to satisfactorily resolve.

The Ship

Ship Yard, Briggate, LS1 6LL
0113 246 8031
www.theshipleeds.co.uk

Thriving under new management, the Ship has become once more some serious competition for Whitelock's. While less distinctively opulent, it shares some of its famous neighbour's architectural features – long, narrow and intimate rooms; sheltered yards which make for natural outdoor drinking spaces. And while the Ship to some extent is the obvious poor relation, it still has plenty to offer – including the splendid Wharfebank Tether Blond when I last called in, the first time I've found it in the city centre.

The Lands Lane end of the alley is topped by an attractive iron sign welcoming you to Ship Yard. From Briggate, a dog-legged blind alley leads to the pub's front door. From here you emerge at the end of an L-shaped bar topped with a decent choice of ales and lagers. Tetley usually features.

Screens of brass piping, oak and tiled counters and etched glass create a series of intimate little booths, the floor is by turns wooden and carpeted, though the chequerboard tiles around the bar can be a little disorientating if encountered while drunk.

If you're searching for true character here, look up. The ceiling features diamond panels of wood lacquered a rich red-brown, while lamps of different styles and brightness are cleverly deployed to effect an impression of warmth. Ornate wooden carvings above the bar offer a further surprise.

A short flight of stairs leads up to the square dining room at the rear, where red U-shaped leather-look seating maximises the use of the space and big mirrors make this poky space seem far bigger.

Here again it's worth looking upwards. An outsize circle has been sculpted into the ceiling to accommodate a much smaller fan. You could probably fit one of the *Titanic's* propellers into this curious space.

Though long gone, the entrance to Briggate's Bay Horse was once below this sign, the former landlord Molineaux's name preserved forever in the brickwork.

Briggate Pubs of Old

Whitelock's and the Ship are both a legacy of the time when alleyways on either side of Briggate hid any number of hotels and alehouses. There were once dozens of these yards, crowded with houses and shops and pubs, parallel alleyways linking the nascent city's major routes.

Around 1850 there were more than 30 pubs – places with fascinating names like The Bull and Mouth, the Blackwell Ox, the Saddle, the Leopard – between the Headrow (then Upperhead and Lowerhead Row) and the river. Some will have opened after the Beerhouse Act of 1830, which halved the duty on beer and led to the number of licensed premises in Leeds doubling to 545 in a decade, though some were much older, like the Old George, name-checked by 17th-century travellers Sir Walter Calverley and Celia Fiennes.

Most of these pubs are gone now, the alleyways bricked up or built over, their utility sacrificed in the name of progress, yet in the topography of the Ship, the Angel, Whitelock's and the Pack Horse can be glimpsed a little of the city's past.

Templar

Templar Street, LS2 7NU
0113 243 0318

Step into the Templar at any time of day and night and you're likely to find it doing good business. By serving a great choice of real ales, offering sensibly-priced spirits, lagers and keg beer, and by showing Sky Sports TV, it manages to pull in a lively cross-section of punters.

With its dark oak beams and more wood panelling than you'd find in the drawing room of a grand country mansion, the Templar exudes something of the feel of a private gentlemen's club. This is particularly so in its square rear snug, where comfy green banquettes, a red-tiled fireplace and displays of old crockery make for a civilised place to drink.

The long main bar is livelier, with its sociable booths, topped by panels of stained glass. Around the walls a series of pictures and displays tell the history of the pub and of the Knights Templar, side by side with posters advertising live sports events and cheap beer promotions. If you're bored, or have nothing better to do and the big match isn't floating your boat, then it's worth boning up on some of the remarkable history represented here.

Though it dates back to the early 19th century the red, green and ivory frontage date back to 1927 and are a legacy of the Templar's time in the Melbourne Brewery chain, though it became part of the Tetley empire in 1964. Tetley and Leeds Brewery products now dominate the bar.

Ruined Spofforth Castle was once a Templar stronghold; in nearby Ribston Chapel the knights are immortalised in stained glass.

The Knights Templar

Founded in the early 12th century, the Knights Templar were among the best known Christian military orders of their time – powerful landowners, feared fighting Crusaders dubbed 'The Army of God' by one early Pope. And though their fame was forged in the Holy Land, it should be no surprise that they are remembered in the name of a Leeds pub and the street it stands upon. The Templars owned more land and property in Yorkshire than in any other English county, including the Temple Newsam estate in east Leeds.

Almost 700 years on from their bloody dissolution which saw many Templars burned at the stake, placenames such as Temple Hirst and Temple Colton tell of their widespread influence; a Templar cross high on the wall of the Pack Horse in Briggate a remnant of the time the original pub here belonged to the Order of St John of Jerusalem – successors to the Templars.

A Templar cross at Briggate's Pack Horse.

Victoria

Great George Street, LS1 3DL
0113 245 1386
www.nicholsonspubs.co.uk

An underground tunnel connects the Town Hall to the splendid Victoria, and was used by judges to get between the courtroom and their hotel room without having to face reprisals in the street outside. It's a legacy of the time when the magnificent Victoria Family and Commercial Hotel – to give it its full title – was a sumptuous working hotel with 27 bedrooms on five floors.

Modern fire regulations and the lack of a lift are among the reasons why these rooms now lie empty and unused. In a city where soulless multi-storey concrete hotels do brisk business, it's a serious shame that visitors are denied the opportunity to spend the night in a place of such character, interest and heritage.

Even so, by simply drinking in the Vic one can get a feel for how it was to be a guest here in its heyday. While walking into most pubs will bring you straight to the bar, here you first enter an ornate hall of swing doors and etched glass, once the hotel's grand lobby.

Its three drinking spaces – lounge bar, Albert's Bar, Bridget's Bar – open off from the main corridor, though only the first of these has an actual bar, a beautiful period piece, with its carved back bar of dark oak and engraved mirrors crowned by distinctive back-lit arches of stained glass. Sturdy pillars spiral from the bar top to the ceiling, where moulded golden rosettes contrast with the terracotta paintwork. Thirties-style light fittings hang overhead, their lamps reflecting from every polished surface.

Along one wall leather-backed booths separated by hinged screens of frosted glass provide intimate places to meet, eat and drink, while long-serving manager Carol Coleman is proud of her line of nine real-ale handpumps. Only Leeds Best and Tetley are ever-presents, while the rest change regularly: 'It keeps the customers interested,' she tells me.

Astonishingly, in the 1970s, the Vic could have been wiped off the map had some philistine town planning scheme been given the go-ahead. Like at the Garden Gate, a public outcry saved the building, and in 1989 it was given special recognition by Leeds Civic Trust for its 'splendid Victorian features and contribution to city life.' That contribution continues daily.

Great George Street

The Vic stands roughly halfway along Great George Street, which offers something of a pub crawl itself. Just beyond its western end, over the little footbridge which crosses the inner ring road is the live music venue **The Well**, and from here head towards town to reach the **George**, a simple traditional alehouse which is a favourite with those visiting either the Magistrates Courts or Leeds General Infirmary.

From here it's on to the more up-market **Veritas**, which combines its role as a real ale gastropub with a working delicatessen. Then there's the **Victoria**, before you reach the Irish themed **O'Neill's** – and then the underground **Carpe Diem**, an occasional bolthole of mine, when I want to watch the cricket in peace. The last pub on Great George Street, before it becomes Merrion Street, used to be called the Courtyard, not least because it has a lovely outdoor drinking space to the rear. So why did someone choose to rename it **A Nation of Shopkeepers**? Anyone?

Fenton

Woodhouse Lane, LS2 3ED

www.myspace.com/thefentonleeds

Despite some concessions to the students – a pool table, a juke box and a breathless programme of live music – the Fenton retains most of its original shape, with two main drinking spaces and a corridor served by a single bar with counters facing each.

It has long been a favourite meeting place for both staff and students. In the 1950s and 1960s, when Leeds University gained a reputation for employing working artists and poets, both to develop their own talents and to enthuse undergraduates with the joy of creativity, the Fenton became the place they would gravitate to, for discussions and poetry readings. Beer, too, obviously.

Wandering into the Fenton, you can easily imagine you have drifted back to those times. With its leather seating, glazed corridor screen, chequerboard tiled floor and old wooden panelling, its faded grandeur seems a better 'fit' with the staff of both the University and Leeds Met, than with the students. You're just as likely to bump into academics discussing their research as undergraduates talking about exams.

As close-knit terraces were cleared and the campus expanded towards the city in the 1960s and 1970s, its growth ended right at the Fenton's back door. The brutalist concrete of the physics department is now just 30 seconds' walk away from the bar. In keeping with a pub where the famous Huntsman motif still hangs outside, you'll often find Tetley bitter here, though the city's

famous ale has now been joined by a host of offcumdens and interlopers. The choice of ales changes almost daily.

The entrance lobby is part tiled, the walls above painted a bloody crimson and stuckled up with posters for live bands. An enclosed yard has been slapped up with murals and decked out with chairs and tables to create an unlikely urban beer garden and a welcome haven for the smokers.

The students often gravitate to a room across the corridor which is dominated by the pool table and juke box, though the Fenton's chief credential as a student pub comes when bands take to the upstairs stage, which is more nights than not. It's the penultimate stop on the Otley Run too, so by the time the fancy-dress pub crawlers reach here, they're usually blathered.

University Pub Crawl

The Leeds University campus, just to the north west of the city centre, is fringed with a little ring of pubs, which form a decent pub crawl all of their own.

Start at the beached barge of the newly refurbished **Dry Dock** directly opposite Leeds Met on Woodhouse Lane, then call in at the **Fenton**, before

passing the Parkinson Tower, to reach the **Eldon**, where Sky TV, decent real ales and cheap and cheerful pub meals make this a popular mainstream lunchtime spot – notably from the engineering department, whose buildings are directly opposite.

A little further on, the **Pack Horse** does great value, simple home-cooking and has a slightly more esoteric range of beers; upstairs is a great, rough-and-ready venue for local bands. Further up the road is the student-themed **Library**, one of the Mitchells and Butler's Scream chain, then take Clarendon

Road and Mount Preston Street to reach the excellent **Faversham** which manages to please both staff and students by offering quality lunchtime dining and then mutating by night into a popular venue for DJs and live music. The live music **Well** is a short hop from here too.

On the campus itself, the student union is home to a number of bars and clubs, the best of which for real ale lovers is the underground **Old Bar**, though the outside drinking space at the **Terrace** makes this a popular summer drinking spot, too.

Pub Crawl Two

The Cross-City Ale Trail

The Cross City Ale Trail cuts east-to-west across the city centre, from the Palace at the historic eastern edge of the city, to the Highland, beyond its original western boundary. While less architecturally significant than some of those on the heritage route, all those on this pub crawl have a great reputation for great real ale – whether that's the wealth of choice on offer at the Palace, the Duck and Drake and Foley's, or the company brewery products of the Angel and the Town Hall Tavern. And at the Fox and Newt, you might even find some beer brewed on the premises – a real rarity in Leeds.

Directions:

The Cross City Ale Trail begins at **The Palace**, just beside Leeds Parish Church on Kirkgate. From here, walk past the church, and cross the road to reach **The Duck and Drake**. Continue towards the city centre, past Leeds markets, crossing Vicar Lane and turning right onto Briggate. Angel Inn Yard and **The Angel** are about 100 yards along here, on your left.

Continue up Angel Inn Yard to reach Lands Lane. Turn right here and then left onto the Headrow, continuing along here to reach first **Mr Foley's** and then the **Town Hall Tavern**. Continue along Westgate, crossing the inner ring road to reach Park Lane, where you will find the **Fox and Newt** on your left.

From here continue out of town for about 100 yards until you reach a flight of steep steps leading down to your left, just before the first block of student residences. At the bottom of the steps turn left for the short walk to the **Highland**.

Approximate total distance: 1.5 miles.

Detours:

With its 'all things to all people' feel, if you wish to extend your pub crawl, it's worth starting your route with a beer or a cocktail at the **Wardrobe** in St

Peter's Square. The route crosses that of the Heritage trail, so the **Ship** and **Whitelock's** are in easy reach, as is the **Pack Horse**. After the Town Hall Tavern, a diversion to York Place would allow you take in **The Old Steps**, a famous old underground bar which is gaining a great reputation for well-kept real ale and home-cooked food. You could finish at the **Queen** on Burley Road, described by writer and historian Barrie Pepper as 'one of the most opulent street corner pubs in the county'. On the opposite corner, the **Corner Café** does fabulous Indian food – and though unlicensed, you can bring in beer from the Queen.

Palace

Kirkgate, LS2 7DJ
0113 244 5882
www.nicholsonspubs.co.uk

Our journey across Leeds begins close to the banks of the Aire, just as the city itself did. The Palace has been a public house since at least 1841, but the building itself dates at least another century, when it was the grand home of timber merchant Edmund Maude.

The arrival of the Leeds-Liverpool canal and Aire and Calder Navigation made this part of the city a thriving hive of commercial activity - and one Palace landlord even built boats behind the pub. The slow, post-war decline of the area might have been terminal, but for the invention of 'city living' and the rapid

Terry Grayson, long-serving licensee of the Palace.

gentrification of this area of neglect. The arrival of new flats, businesses and hotels have given this great old pub a fresh constituency.

It is every bit the classic alehouse, a U-shaped arrangement of rooms clustered around a central bar topped with a tempting and ever-changing selection of beers. The furniture is by turns leather sofas and wooden-topped stools, gnarled wooden tables and barrels, the decor burgundy, chocolate and white, and the main bar area dominated by a great old clock and a brick fireplace. Out back is an attractive courtyard area, lit by a hundreds of tiny bulbs strung above it like a blanket of stars.

At the front, a paved area affords yet more outdoor drinking space, decorated with attractive hanging baskets. For traffic arriving in the city over Crown Point Bridge, the whitewashed Palace with its green and gold livery and colourful floral displays, must be a very welcome sight.

It is part of the same Mitchell's and Butler's chain which includes two other classic Leeds pubs in this guide, the Victoria and the Scarbrough. All three boast long-serving licensees – Terry Grayson has been a steady hand on the tiller down here for well over a decade.

THE PALACE

Originally a private house of the mid 18th century with railings to the front and long rear gardens extending to the River Aire, The Palace was once the home of Leeds timber merchant Edmund Maude.

It was first recorded as an Inn in 1841 when the landlord was Henry Teall, a boatbuilder of Leeds bridge, this may explain the long passage which runs toward the river from the old cellars.

In 1874 The Palace passed to a family called Castelow who made beer in the Inn's Brewhouse & over the years the inn was extended to take in an adjacent cottage & Pawnbroker's shop.

Early History

Some of the key moments in the city's history are illustrated on a signboard just outside the Palace. When it was first built, the building stood outside the city boundary, whose eastern limits were marked by the East Bar Stone, which can still be seen set into the wall of the nearby Parish church.

EAST BAR

This ancient stone marked the eastern boundary of the medieval town of Leeds.

The earliest references to the city are in the eighth-century writings of Bede who refers to Loidis, though revered 18th-century historian Ralph Thoresby asserts the town had Roman origins.

After the Norman conquest – once William had laid waste to the north – the area was bestowed on Norman baron Ilbert de Laci, and as well as 'Ledes' being mentioned in the Domesday book of 1086, nearby settlements such as Ermelei (Armley) and Hedingleia (Headingley) were already established too.

By the time of Elizabeth I, a map of the town shows a layout of early streets – Kirkgate, Lowerhead Row, Briggate and Vicar Lane – whose geometry remains largely unchanged today.

Duck and Drake

Kirkgate, LS2 7DR

0113 245 5432

www.duckndrake.co.uk

The walk up Kirkgate edges us ever closer to the railway line, and into that slightly grimy twilight zone between the Corn Exchange and the back end of the market.

By comparison to the Palace, the hanging baskets at the Duck and Drake are fallow, its reputation a little intimidating, its exterior less strikingly pretty, its clientele more alternative – and you might easily scurry past.

Yet to do so would be to miss out on one of Leeds's very few unspoiled, no-nonsense city alehouses, with two high-ceilinged, bare-floorboarded rooms serving well-kept real ales in a genuine, lively tavern atmosphere.

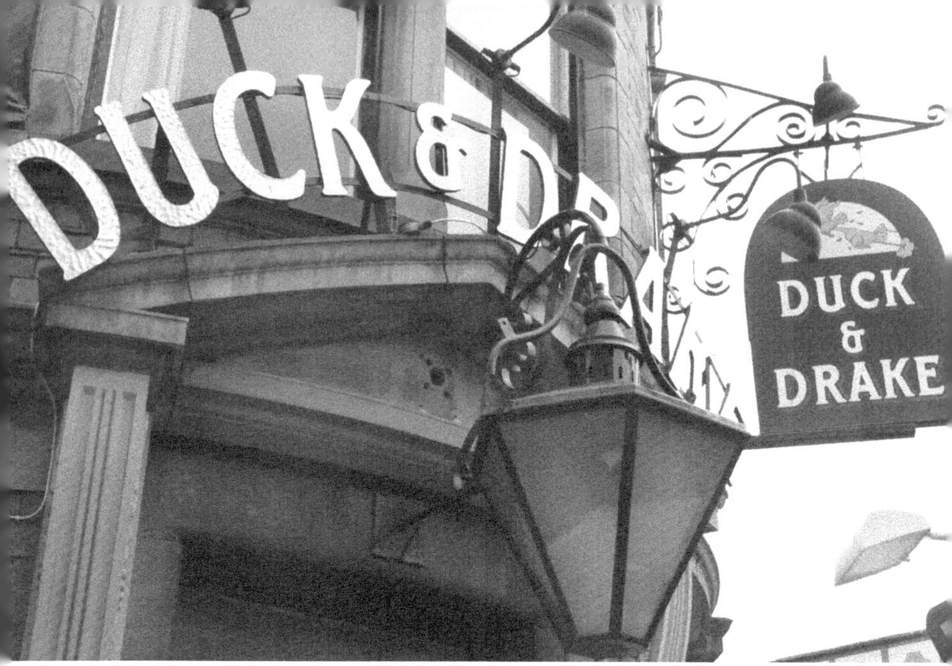
DUCK & DRAKE

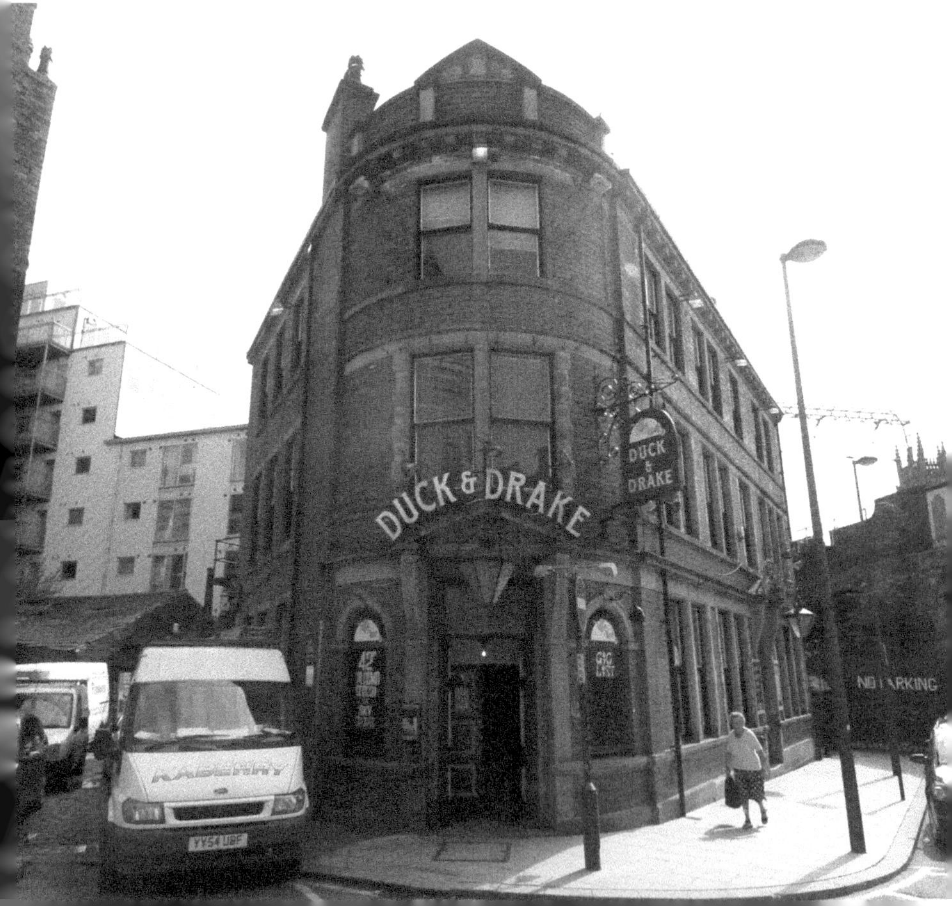
DUCK & DRAKE
DUCK & DRAKE

The former Scottish and Newcastle pub has long had a reputation for its variety of ales, and an ever-changing blackboard is chalked up with the latest arrivals, though curiously all the handpumps are on the side of the bar facing into the pub's lounge. You could call into the taproom and think that real ale was off the agenda altogether.

There's a curious native American theme to some of the decor in the taproom, including a sizeable Red Indian head-dress. This is maintained in the tiny beer garden to the rear where an incredible mural depicts the mythical otherworldly landscape of the Wyrd Wood, where snowbound peaks rise above dense woodland, naked hairy-armpitted women ride wolves and wild horses; owls and boars and half-caribou-half-men creatures emerge from the foliage.

The draughtsmanship is splendid, if the subject matter a little perverse. The artist, a chap who goes simply by the name of 'Trot', is apparently working up designs to cover the entire wall space of this tiny yard, where smokers, drinkers, art lovers can only wonder at the strange workings of this talented artist's mind.

Though there has been a pub here for 200 years, it has traded under different names, including The Horse and Groom and The Brougham's Arms, before settling on the current name as recently as 1985. It re-opened in September last year after a short closure and a change of management which has now brought it into the same stable as the World's End at Knaresborough and Harrogate's Blues Bar.

Music Images

The larger of the two rooms at the Duck and Drake is a regular concert venue and across its walls can be found a fascinating collection of vintage posters advertising gigs by the Stones, the Who and T Rex. A giant mural around the bar features legends like Axl Rose, Stevie Wonder, Elvis, Clapton, Page and Plant.

The concert room at the **Grove** is another with a great selection of music photographs, while to drink at **Mojo** is to bask in the reflected cool of Bob Marley and Neil Young, Pink Floyd and Patti Smith.

But perhaps the city's most distinctive collection of music photography is on permanent display in the Refectory at the **University of Leeds**. Remarkable not least because the vast majority of these were taken in the Refectory itself, a legacy of the time when acts like Led Zeppelin, Pink Floyd, the Rolling Stones, Bob Marley, Elton John and the Clash included this cavernous student venue on their national tours. And on Valentine's Day 1970, the Who's seminal album *Live At Leeds* was recorded there too.

Ian Dury, Paul McCartney and Slade are among the host of acts whose performances at Leeds University are celebrated in the Refectory's permanent exhibition of photographs.

Angel

Angel Inn Yard, LS1 6LN

0113 245 1428

If ever a pub could be described as having two personalities, then it would probably be the Angel. It had been closed as licensed premises for many years when it was re-opened by Samuel Smith's in the 1990s – a watch repairer and a tailoring business had shared the building in the meantime.

If nothing else, Sam's brings two guarantees to a pub – decent real ale and low prices. And, in a similar phenomenon to The Wetherspoon's Effect, this pulls in those eager to drink proper cask beer, and those who will drink anything, just so long as it's cheap.

Which all makes for a very mixed clientele. And if you happen upon Angel Inn Yard some afternoons you might easily wonder if you have stumbled on the last drinking den of the lost, the disappointed and dispossessed. It can be certainly be rather lively down here. Yet the fine dining and genteel atmosphere of the Angel's upstairs lounge pulls in a quite different crowd, in search of relaxation and quality, food and conversation.

Yet it all works remarkably well, not least because – unlike the Ship and Whitelock's, whose essential alleyway footprint it shares – the Angel is on three levels.

Inside at ground level, elderly chaps ekeing out their pensions gather at the main bar. The decor is spartan, utilitarian, with its wooden floors and benches.

Upstairs it is like a completely different place. With its leather armchairs, black and white photographs of the city, and tartan carpets, one could almost be in the sumptuous drawing room of a gentleman's club. A second bar serves the whole range of Sam Smith's products, while menus on every table emphasise that this is also very much the dining area.

Only in the yard outside and in the barrel-vaulted cellars, where the toilets are situated, do these two rather different groups of drinkers ever meet.

Samuel Smith's Brewery

At more than 250 years old, Sam Smith's is one of the oldest family-owned breweries in the world and one of the few remaining large independents in the UK.

It is also among the biggest companies of any kind not to have a website, this a measure of the Tadcaster brewery's determined – and occasionally quirky – independence. By contrast, nearby John Smith's, which started as the result of a disagreement in the Smith family, is now part of the giant Scottish and Newcastle group.

Sam Smith's trades on tradition, with the Old Brewery water drawn from a well sunk more than 200 years ago, a strain of yeast dating back 100 years, hand-weighed hops and fermentation in slate Yorkshire Squares.

Its 200-or-so pubs, mostly in Yorkshire, but some spread around the UK, including several in London, sell only Sam Smith's products, but the trade-off for this lack of choice is that they charge rock-bottom prices. And no less an authority than world-famous beer writer Roger Protz rates Sam Smith's malty, butterscotchy Old Brewery Pale Ale highly enough to give it a place in his book *300 Beers To Try Before You Die*.

Mr Foley's

Headrow, LS1 5RG

0113 242 9674

mrfoleyscaskalehouse.co.uk

With its great choice of beers and benign, comfortable surroundings, this is fast becoming one of the great city centre alehouses. It makes the most of its opulent surroundings, doing full justice to a 100-year-old building which was once the elegant home of Pearl Assurance. A statue of its founder Patrick James Foley stands high on the building, flanked by two griffins.

What such a building said about the company was a statement every bit as

telling as those which are made about the Victorian city by the grandeur of the library, art gallery and forbidding Town Hall, directly opposite. Its conversion into a pub was both tasteful and sensitive. Wooden staircases, an attractive mezzanine, plush leather sofas and a grand oak-panelled bar blend perfectly with those original features – sculpted beams, ornate plaster mouldings – which remain.

Foley's manager Dean Pugh.

Dramatic arched windows fringed by heavy drapes afford a view over the traffic and shoppers on East Parade, giving drinkers that comfortable feeling of superiority of knowing that one would rather be inside than out.

Foley's is owned by York Brewery, and their beers predominate on the long bar top. It was their session beer, the pale, softly bitter and refreshing Guzzler, that I was drinking on my most recent visit, though the choice changes almost daily. Guest ales from around the country, plus an interesting choice of lagers and world beers, add further to the mix. The food is simple, wholesome and unpretentious – sandwiches, burgers, sausages, chillis and steaks.

The building's conversion did allow some notable concessions to the 21st century, like the multi-screen Sky TV system which burbles away incessantly to itself most of the time, but draws in a good crowd for the big games. And the illuminated Krombacher sign high on one internal wall does look less in keeping with its surroundings than the posters promoting beer old and new.

But I suspect that from his lofty perch, overlooking a fast-changing world, even Mr Foley himself might approve.

Martin Kellaway at Wharfebank Brewery.

Wharfebank Brewery

By the summer of 2011, little more than a year into its operation, Wharfebank Brewery was already a serious player on the local scene – and a popular sight on the bar at Foley's too.

Boss Martin Kellaway knows the industry inside out, after graduating from the Bass management programme and taking up sales and marketing roles with both Fullers and Caledonian. Cally's takeover by Dutch giant Heineken gave him the opportunity to walk away with a redundancy cheque and strike out on his own.

And from an industrial unit in Pool, Wharfebank is turning out a cracking little range of real ales. Tether Blond is sharp, pale and citric; full-bodied coffee-ish Camfell Flame is darker, a deep ruby red born of the amber and crystal malts used in the brew; Slinger's Gold has a rounded passion fruit taste imparted by a trio of American hops. This regular roster is filled out with month-long specials.

Wharfebank's first pub, the revived Fleece in Otley, gave Martin his first opportunity to line up all the brews on one bar – and it's already proving a winner..

Town Hall Tavern

Westgate, LS1 2RA

0113 244 0765

www.townhalltavernleeds.co.uk

The sign outside declares that the Town Hall Tavern was established in 1926, but its current look is entirely 2011.

In fact, if any of the lawyers, police, journalists – and criminals – who frequented this place during its first 60 years of life were to call in today, they would find it quite unrecognisable. Its proximity to the courts and to the legal practices of Park Square have always made the THT a haven for those who had business with the law, whichever side of it they happened to be on.

I'm old enough to remember its nooks and crannies, screens and baffles

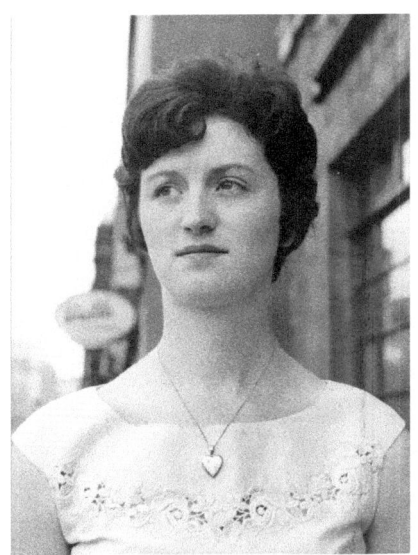

which lent an appropriately intimate feel. Former barmaid Mary Ruane recalls that the customers generally divided into two, the law in one room, the accused in the other. Private and occasionally conspiratorial business could be safely conducted here.

Mary Ruane pulled pints at the Town Hall Tavern in the 1960s.

63

Like the Old Unicorn at Bramley, the THT was once in the ownership of the Dickensian-sounding pub company Musgrave and Sagar. The two were snapped up by the expanding Timothy Taylor pub empire some years ago.

An open-plan design was adopted during the 1980s and the latest re-fit has seen it smartened up, the menu jolted sharply up-market, and a cocktail list and excellent bottled beer menu introduced. The floor is dark-lacquered parquet, the paintwork grey-green, ivory and deep navy blue.

A short bar juts out into the room, topped by pumps dispensing Taylor's flagship brands Golden Best, Landlord and Ram Tam, while prints around the wall play to the legal theme.

Timothy Taylor Brewery

Shortly after celebrating its 150th birthday in 2008, Keighley's famous Timothy Taylor brewery announced a three-year development programme which includes a £2.7 million extension with six additional fermenters. Now complete, this investment says much about the confidence of this family-run company, and the continued high regard which drinkers have for their beers.

Timothy Taylor continue to use the same Knowle Spring Pennine water as their founder did to create their fabulous range of beers: nicely-balanced traditional Best Bitter, their light-tasting session beer Golden Best, dark winter warmer Ram Tam, and their rich smooth Dark Mild.

Which is to say nothing of fruity, juicy, earthy, Timothy Taylor Landlord, a British brewing classic whether in bottle or on draught and a champion beer of Britain a record four times in CAMRA's 40-year history. It's Madonna's favourite beer too, apparently.

Fox and Newt

Burley Street LS3 1LD
0113 245 4527

It's an ill wind that blows nobody any good – and the gas explosion which tore through the Rutland Hotel in 1979 may have wreaked local devastation, but it ultimately brought a major benefit. When it re-opened as the Fox and Newt, the drinking area had been expanded into a neighbouring shop, doubling the floor space.

The Rutland was always something of an oddity, having opened in the early 19th century as a one-bedroomed hotel – the smallest in Britain. The name reflected its size, or lack of it, and can still be seen in the stonework above the front door.

The pub's catchment area has changed beyond all recognition since the war. The residential area it once served has seen terraces cleared and the inner ring road slice through its heartland. Though some homes remain and there is a high-rise estate beyond its back door, the Fox's position outside the city's main circuit, reduces its potential for casual passing trade. A couple of fast food outlets next door, and a small fleet of minicabs which seem always parked outside, don't exactly help the image.

With its alehouse atmosphere and no-nonsense range of products – some brewed on the premises – this has never really been a student pub, despite new accommodation blocks next door. But a link-up with the Pack Horse, near the University, and the re-opening of its upstairs function toom, has seen the Fox and Newt revive its credentials as a live music venue. A Sunday night comedy club is also starting to pull in the punters.

From busy Burley Road you step into a very basic one-room drinking house, which has been much cleaned up and brightened recently, yet it retains the feel of an old-fashioned boozer where everyone is welcome. The area to the left of the small bar is dominated by a pool table; to the right is a raised drinking space, slightly more intimate than the rest of the open-plan interior.

It combines traditional elements such as stained glass above the bar, with 21st-century necessities such as a big-screen plasma TV. Its menu offers a big selection of cheap-and-cheerful pub meals, along with some surprising departures from the norm like a pizza with black pudding or a hummous and olive sandwich. And if you like your old-school puddings like jam sponge and spotted dick, this could be a good place to come too.

The Fox and Newt was once a favourite haunt of the *Yorkshire Evening Post* football team, and my colleague Darryl Wills once persuaded the landlord to brew our own beer. The pub showed the video of our Media Cup Final demolition of the *Northern Echo* on the big screen while we made equally short work of 'Darryl's Barrel'. I scored two, if you're interested.

Anna Stewart, brewster at the Felon and Firkin during its pre-Millennium heyday.

Leeds brewpubs

The Fox and Newt is perhaps the best-known brewpub in Leeds, though a slightly chequered history over the last 10 years or so has seen the underground brewhouse periodically mothballed and then re-opened. Different owners have each tried to put their own stamp on the product and I remember trying a luminous green ale here once, years ago. It's currently under the stewardship of brewers Michael Wynnyczuk and Dawn Collins, and on my most recent visit I enjoyed a pint of their rich, dry, slightly sweet Brickyard Ale.

The rapid expansion of the Firkin chain in the 1990s made brewpubs fleetingly common in city centres across the country. Leeds had two, though the microbrewery at the Felon and Firkin in Great George Street (now O'Neill's) also supplied the Feast and Firkin on Woodhouse Moor (now The Library).

There was also briefly a brewery in the unlikely venue of the Hollywood Bowl at Kirkstall, but that has long gone, leaving here and the Brewery Tap as the city's only two remaining brewpubs.

The Highland

Cavendish Street, LS3 1LY
0113 242 8592

With the city end of Burley Road fast becoming the new heartland for student accommodation the Highland is ideally placed to keep this new population fed and watered.

Like the Fox and Newt, it is a pub which has had a chequered recent past, particularly in its time as a leased house. The business model for leaseholder pubs often seems flawed to me, chiefly because it gives the pub companies, as owners, no real imperative for their houses to succeed. The risk is disproportionately weighted onto the licensee, who has to pay for the lease, pay the rent and pay for the beer – all these to the pub company – and try make a living at the same time.

While the massive buying power of these companies means they can screw down a great deal on beer at the brewery gate, their discounts aren't always passed on to their lessees. Thousands of people, attracted by the idea of running a pub, seduced by the promise of it being their own business, have blundered into bars like these, all bright eyed and optimistic – and failed. Many, sad to say, have lost everything.

It was sad to see the Highland lurch from one crisis to the next. To be honest I'd actually given it up for lost, during a long year when it stood empty and abandoned.

But its leasehold days are gone and under the new ownership of Richard Mollitt, this great little two-room alehouse has undergone a serious refit and is once again making its presence felt.

It's an architectural curiosity, formed from knocking two terraced houses together – though the rest of them are now long gone. But approaching along Cavendish Street you do get a sense of its unlikely geometry, a graceful wedge of red brick which tapers to bay windows just a metre and a half across.

The table in this window, and the red leather seating which follows the curving contours of the wall, were once the preserve of a small hardy band of Evening Post journalists, who would wander up here for a beer and a lunchtime sandwich, and roll gently back down hill to work an hour or more later

Two of them eventually bought a bar of their own, the excellent little Old Steps in York Place, so naturally the YEP crowd tends to congregate there these days. But with something like 4,000 students living within a few hundred yards, Richard has a new captive clientele to look after. After stints at the Eldon in Woodhouse and the Three Horseshoes in Headingley, he has the know-how to crack the student market.

From the cobbled end of Cavendish Street you enter the narrow main bar area, newly scrubbed and repainted; to the right is a smaller, squarer snug, dominated by a big screen TV above the fireplace.

The bar itself is a little gem, an elegant free-standing sideboard of curved and panelled mahogany like something you might expect to find on a twenties steamer on the Nile. It's topped by three real ale handpumps; the choice changes regularly.

There are some nice touches. An old carpet has been lifted to reveal an attractive tiled floor; plaid bar stools and tartan cushions and curtains play to the Highland theme.

The Royal Park.

Student pubs

As well as those around the two main University campuses and those on the Otley Run, there are a host of Leeds pubs which rely on students as a source of income. The largest pub in the city is the cavernous **Royal Park** in Hyde Park, an area whose terraced houses have proved popular for student lets. It offers pool tables and live big screen sport, the latter also an attraction at Aussie-themed **Walkabout**. **Oceana** on the side of the Merrion Centre, **Yates's** and **Space** are all top student hang-outs too.

Pub Crawl Three

City Centre Bar Crawl

While new and interesting bars have opened up right across the centre of Leeds over the past 20 years, this explosion in the city's drinking culture is especially concentrated in two areas – one either side of the Grand Theatre, the other around Call Lane.

This pub crawl visits both, and includes venues whose business is built around foreign beers and those for whom the cocktail is king.

It is by no means an exhaustive trail. Bars like Mook, just off Duncan Street, and Pin in Dock Street failed to make the final cut – but hopefully the seven selected here offer a representative flavour of 21st-century bar culture in the cosmopolitan city of Leeds.

Directions:

The **Reliance** is in North Street, just north of the Leeds Inner Ring Road. Turn left out of the front door, cross the motorway bridge to reach New Briggate and after 100 metres turn right into Cross Belgrave Street for **Sandinista!** From here return to New Briggate, but immediately go left into Merrion Street, where **Mojo** is on the left. Then it's back to New Briggate, turning left towards the city centre you reach **North Bar**, before continuing along Briggate to its junction with Boar Lane and Duncan Street, where you turn left, and then right into Call Lane, where **Jake's Bar** is next door to **Oporto**. Continue to The Calls, where you turn left, and after 100 metres **Aire Bar** is on your right.
Approximate total distance: 0.8 miles.

Detours:

There are sufficient pubs and bars on this route that, with a little careful planning, you could plan a route to rival the Otley Run, but with considerably less of the inconvenience of a long hike.

You could start lower down North Street, where there was a string of pubs on this stretch between the city and Sheepscar, serving the folk who lived in the tightly-packed rows of terraced housing nearby. Of these, only the famous old **Eagle Tavern** remains, a fine Georgian building and one of the oldest unaltered pubs in the whole city.

The **Wrens**, **Verve**, **Reform**, **Sela**, **Norman** and **Neon Cactus** are all in close proximity to the main route, while short detours could include the splendidly cool **Milo** and **Mook**. And if you fancy ending your night of beer and cocktails with an actual beer cocktail – then after Aire Bar cross the river to find **Pin** in Dock Street, where they are something of a speciality.

The Reliance

North Street, LS2 7PN
0113 295 6060
www.the-reliance.co.uk

The laid-back Reliance is a perennial favourite on the Leeds bar scene. A little off the beaten track in North Street, its quality beer and proper pub food continues to attract a big following.

The Reli's attractive frontage of tall windows curving around a street corner, sits some 50 yards beyond the inner ring road. It has a cool feel of faded elegance to it, with its high ceilings, gnarled bare floorboards and simple colour scheme of creams, deep reds and greens. Drinkers and diners share big, solid oak tables and chairs, while a room to the right of the main entrance has some comfy leather sofas too. Flickering tea lights add to the intimacy of a bar which is as much at home to big lively groups of friends and colleagues as it is to lovers

enjoying a first kiss in the candlelight.

The menu combines comfort food favourites like sausages and mash and battered haddock, with some more less-obvious alternatives – poached hake, kedgeree, leg of duck.

It isn't obviously passed by shoppers or pedestrians and is not easily driven to unless you know precisely where you're going. I'm sure that plenty who tread the popular circuit of North Bar, Reform, Mojo, Verve and Sandinista! never actually find their way here.

Which is a shame in some ways, but a blessing in others, as the Reli tends to attract a slightly older crowd, often those who spend the whole evening there, rather than bar-hopping with the rest. In every sense, the Reliance is ever-so-slightly set apart from everything else.

And while those other bars get a fair supply of students, the Reli attracts the postgraduates, the lecturers and the University staff. They're probably quite happy to find in the Reliance a reliable hideaway from the undergraduates.

Dining pubs

Pubs have long been a popular fall-back for those looking to eat out, whether for a sturdy, reasonably-priced dinner, or a simple lunchtime refuelling stop. And while many simply offer the cook-to-formula menus of the big pub chains, Leeds still has plenty of pubs employing proper chefs who are proud to offer seriously good food. The **Reliance**, the **Cross Keys**, **Veritas** and the **Adelphi** are among city-centre dining favourites.

In recent years, the explosion of gastropubs – plus

the growing awareness of beer, rather than wine, as an ideal match for food – has extended beyond all measure the range of dining options available to pubgoers, who are increasingly receptive to the idea of pairing different food with specially-selected beers.

Sandinista!

Cross Belgrave Street, LS2 8JP

0113 305 0372

www.sandinistaleeds.co.uk

Punk passed me by. I was the wrong age and too hooked up on Zeppelin and Floyd to be moved by Siouxsie or the Sex Pistols.

Sandinista! is a small homage to the Clash, though its name is equally reflective of the Nicaraguan freedom movement which inspired the album title. Eight years on, it remains true to its owners' Bohemian vision of an ethically driven, ethnically diverse business, the juices Cuban, the coffees Nicaraguan, and Fairtrade tea, sugar and hot chocolate.

For similar right-on reasons, products you won't find here are the Bacardi brands – Martini, Bombay Sapphire, Jack Daniels – as well as Coca-Cola and anything from whaling countries Japan, Norway and Iceland.

Sandinista! opens mid-afternoon, but it's better after dark when they light the candles and the huge picture windows offer a surprising panorama of floodlit buildings, hypnotic tail lights and twinkling tungsten.

The central bar serves two distinct drinking spaces one of which transforms magically into a music and dance venue late on, the tables whisked down through a trap door while the DJ booth is cranked into life. There's live music twice a week too.

In keeping with its positioning as a Cantina Bar, the food is mostly tapas, the fridges stocked with overseas beers, some Iberian, some American. Even on Sundays, when they do a 'home comforts' menu of traditional food for anyone who overdid it the night before, the choices are given a Spanish twist.

The draught beers are some interesting alternatives to the usual staples – Sagres lager from Portugal and a Sierra Nevada pale ale when I called in, late on a dark February night. It was also a perfect night to make acquaintance with their warm winter honey cider, an addictive, soothing, almost cough-mixturey melange of warm apples, vanilla and marzipan. I asked for the recipe, but they were giving nothing away.

Scott Tyrer and Rebecca Eite at Sandinista!

The Wrens

The Wrens, in Merrion Street, is just around the corner from Sandinista! and hugely popular with theatre-goers who find this the ideal pre- and post-performance watering hole. It suffered a little during the major building works which have transformed the Grand Theatre, but with that now complete, it has come into its own once again.

It is named after founder Alfred Wren, this once-common method of naming pubs applies also to a few others in this guide including the Scarbrough and Whitelock's – and more recently, Jake's Bar.

It serves a great choice of real ales – Landlord, Black Sheep and Leeds Pale on my last visit – and until recently was run by the same family concern which looks after the splendid Chemic Tavern on Woodhouse Moor. Theatrical memorabilia predominates.

Mojo

Merrion Street, LS1 6PQ

0113 244 6387

www.mojobar.co.uk

Mojo boss Mal Evans.

If you're looking for draught beer, don't bother with Mojo, which doesn't sell a single one, not even a draught lager. And if you like your bars to look good from the outside, or have stunning panoramic views from their front windows, you'd probably be best to give this place a miss as well, given its location down the curiously narrow, lightless and slightly seedy end of Merrion Street, which serves as a handy ratrun for traffic on the city loop.

And yet to leave Mojo out from any trawl around the licensed premises of Leeds would be to omit a bar which over the past 15 years has helped to re-define the city's whole drinking culture. With its fridges stuffed with an exciting choice of beers, its cocktail list brimming with old favourites and new

creations, and its endlessly fascinating collection of rock photographs, louche-living Mojo remains a great place to visit.

Mojo combines something of the slightly shabby chic of a New York drinking den with the musical memorabilia of a Hard Rock Café, and for me at least, its compelling combination of music, cocktails, lager and sheer atmosphere makes it the daddy of the Leeds bar scene. I like it best just after opening, when you can get served without having to fight through the crowds to reach the bar, when you can find a seat, or wander around those fantastic photographs, listen to the music and enjoy a quiet conversation. As evening drifts into night the bar becomes louder, the soundtrack harder, the pace of life that bit more frantic.

Boss Mal Evans is the cocktail guru, and has added some distinctive signature drinks to a list which also features classics like the Rum Punch and the Caipirinha.

And for all its lack of draught beer, Mojo packs some curious and revelatory choices into its sizeable fridge space. Crisp and characterful Bernard Pilsner from the Czech Republic, rich and potent Alhambra Reserva from Spain and mellow citric Blue Moon wheat beer from Colorado – complete with a slice of

orange jammed into the neck – are all drinks I made my first acquaintance with here.

New Briggate Bar Scene

While North and Mojo have redefined the New Briggate drinking scene, at least three other bars have joined the party, each of them distinctive and worthy of further exploration.

Next door to Mojo is **Verve**, stylish and cool with some fabulous beers, including a clutch of worthily-famous Belgians. Beyond that is the seventies-themed **Reform**, which manages to combine being a quiet chilled-out after-work drinking den, with being a jumping late-night party place. Once a month it stays open all night.

A couple of doors down from North is the dimly-lit stairwell which leads to the subterranean **Sela Bar**, where a short bar counter is crammed with an excitingly continental range of beers including one peach and one strawberry last time I was in. Plain wooden furniture stretches along both walls, leading to a small stage at the opposite end to the bar where live acts entertain the crowd in this artsy underground bar.

Greg Mulholland's Otley Pub Crawl

Leeds North West MP Greg Mulholland is Chairman of Parliament's Save the Pub Group – and a stout defender of pub culture. Greg has suggested these 14 pubs as a comprehensive ramble around his home town.

It starts at The **Fleece** in Westgate, beautifully restored as Wharfebank's brewery tap, before crossing the road to reach the cosy, one-roomed **Cross Pipes**.

The **Black Horse**, a 17th-century coaching inn, is reckoned by some to be Otley's finest building and offers both a carvery and bed and breakfast. With its emphasis on simple pub food and Yorkshire real ales The **Bay Horse** in the market place is a 'proper boozer'. The **Black Bull** is the oldest in the town, drunk dry by Cromwell's troops on the eve of the Battle of Marston Moor.

Beside each other in Kirkgate, The **Red Lion** and **Whitaker's** are lively, traditional ale houses, the **Ring O'Bells** an open plan pub tucked away in New Market Street. The **Bowling Green** has been reborn as a Wetherspoon's; the splendid **Old Cock** free house in Crossgate looks like it has been there forever, not just since 2010.

Bondgate's stone-built **Rose and Crown** is popular for food and discos, the nearby **Junction** has up to 11 different real ales and dozens of malt whiskies. The **White Swan** in Boroughgate is an 18th-century coaching house, whose rear yard hosts morris dancing during Otley Folk Festival; The **Manor** in Walkergate is a Thwaites' pub popular with folkies all year round.

North

New Briggate, LS1 6NU

0113 242 4540

www.northbar.com

North is an institution on the city bar scene. A catalyst for developing this once-neglected part of town as a haven of bar culture, this long, narrow, often rather cramped bar can still spring a surprise with its choice of beers, and is always worth a visit.

It is the range of beers which has made this place such a favourite on the circuit. The selection, both on the bar and in the amply-stocked double-fronted fridges behind, is refreshed on a regular basis, though you can generally expect

to find lagers from Germany, Italy and the Low Countries, plenty of bottled beers from around the globe, draught Krieks and Framboises.

The décor is deceptively simple, with sage green walls and a parquet floor, leather stools against a purple-fronted bar. Around the walls are dotted a range of original artworks – North doubles as a gallery, allowing local artists to show off their skills.

Glass globe lights suspended over the bar add a warm glow to a room lit by a two rails of spotlights, though a little of the natural light from Briggate penetrates to the back of the long bar. Perhaps a little spartan and soulless when empty, it packs a great atmosphere once the beer starts flowing and the noise levels increase.

Despite the huge changes all around in the decade and more since North first opened its doors, it remains unspoiled, unpretentious, and true to its mission of bringing great beer to the people of Leeds.

North Bar Group

North was the original member of North Bar group, which trades on a mix of cosmopolitan beers and an atmosphere of relaxed cool in a few select venues across the city.

It started with North Bar in Briggate – now simply **North** – the first bar in the UK to offer lovely Erdinger on draught; the first in Leeds to serve draught Brooklyn. It expanded via the **Cross Keys** the group's only south-of-the-river outpost, and the small but beautifully formed **Further North** in Chapel Allerton. **Alfred** in Meanwood is the latest addition to the chain, and the **Reliance** in North Street was once a stablemate too.

Each – even the tiny bar counter at Further North – serves British ales, and a range of authentic quality beers both on draught and in bottle, drawn from every corner of the brewing world. A tie-up with Rooster's means that beers from the Knaresborough beer can usually be found on their bars.

Jake's Bar

Call Lane, LS1 7BT
0113 243 1110
www.jakesbar.co.uk

One storey below street level, cool, chic and intriguing, the formula of good beer, quality food, and outstanding cocktails has made Jake's a bar which others measure themselves against – particularly those here in Call Lane, cocktail-central on the Leeds map.

Sculpted around the charismatic personality of renowned mixologist Jake Burger, the bar which bears his name remains the number one place for inventive, colourful mixed drinks, despite Jake's own departure for the award-winning Portobello Star in London.

The eponymous Jake Burger doing his stuff.

A short dog-legged flight of stairs leads down to the cavernous main bar, where plain white walls, long leather sofas and some surprising Yorkshire stone cladding  contrast with the brightly-lit display of colourful spirit bottles behind the bar.

The drinks menu is a small booklet covering all the major bases from 19th century Manhattans and Mint Juleps, through to the more recent Mojitos and Caipirinhas. Look hard and you'll find that even the much-reviled Pina Colada has been given a 21st-century image makeover too.

Away from this open-plan main room, some more secluded spots in the bowels of the bar, under and behind the staircase, offer more intimate and companionable drinking spaces, the white-ceramic brickwork strangely reminiscent of the London underground or some pre-war public toilets.

Cocktail culture

According to the drinks menu at Jake's, mankind has been mixing spirits since about an hour after we discovered the process of distillation. And though the word 'cocktail' has been around for more than 200 years, it was really only in the 1970s and 80s that they became part of the mainstream drinking culture in the UK – when places like Leeds's much-missed diners Damn Yankee and Ike's Bistro began offering their customers something alternative to wine and cold beer.

The colourful swizzle sticks, mini-sparklers and paper parasols are now consigned to the dustbin of history – except for the purposes of post-ironic retro-cool – while dreadful names like Sex On The  Beach and Sloe Comfortable Screw have been thankfully abandoned too.

Instead, cocktails have become a serious business, and plenty of city bars now offer comprehensive lists, while mixologists like Mal Evans and Sam Fish at **Mojo**, Ricco Dynan and Foxy at **Jake's**, Dan Andrews at **Neon Cactus** and Tom Hepworth at **Epernay** compete for prominence by scouring the world for exciting new spirits, introducing ever-more-subtle variations on familiar recipes and demonstrating their delicate magical alchemy with masterclasses for their customers.

For me, though, you can't beat a good Bloody Mary, really sharp, really dirty, really sour.

Oporto

Call Lane, LS1 7BT
0113 243 4008
www.oportobar.co.uk

Lovely draught Blue Moon, clovey, cloudy and creamy, with its obligatory slice of orange, is one of the signature beers at this long-running city favourite, right next door to Jake's and owned by the same company – but back up at street level.

The formula is very simple – bare floorboards, red brick, red lights, red candles, crimson sofas, terracotta plasterwork, and lots of music.

Oporto has always felt a little as though it were Mojo's southside sibling, a half mile down Briggate, but with the same essential recipe for success. There are some differences of emphasis – Oporto offers draught beer, Mojo's cocktail list is more impressive, but they are cut from the same cloth.

From Call Lane you step directly into the main bar, where tall bar stools, plain wooden chairs, and soft low sofas offer a range of seating options. A gap in the wall leads through to a second drinking space with its own bar.

From industrial pillars at either end of the room hang menacing racks of giant black speakers. It can get pretty loud in here, and rather lively.

Art's Café

A fixture on the Leeds dining and drinking scene for two decades, Art's continues to offer quality food and beer, on a street where it faces stiff competition from the likes of **Jake's**, **Norman**, **Call Lane Social** and **Neon Cactus**.

There's something faintly NYC about it. With its laid-back café ambience and its big picture windows onto the busy street, you half expect a yellow cab or crosstown bus to pull up outside.

The area nearest the door is largely for the drinkers, with bare floorboards, plain wooden tables and lovely draught Moretti on the bar.

A couple of steps lead up to the coralled dining area in the rear. There are lots of steak and fish choices here, though the wealth of vegetarian choices feels more at one with its artsy, bohemian feel.

Aire Bar

The Calls, LS2 7EW
0113 2455500
www.airebar.co.uk

As a teenager I remember the Calls being a dreary and lonesome place of derelict warehouses, wasteland and dingy, twilight zone businesses clinging to life – and after dark somewhere you would only visit with sinister intent. The notion of sitting on a riverside terrace drinking Belgian wheat beer or a Yorkshire real ale and admiring the view was almost so fanciful you would scarcely have entertained it.

So Aire Bar represented a revolution in the local eating and drinking scene when it first opened as Sparrow's Wharf some 15 years ago. It sent out a clear message that the resurgence of this end of town was really under way; that it could be genuinely pleasant to drink beside the River Aire; that the city living revolution was real.

Even so, the high-rise apartment complexes which it looks out upon, which dominate the southern riverbank from the millennium footbridge to Crown Point Bridge, were but a gleam in the developer's eye back then. There were plans to be approved, buildings to clear, a sceptical public to be convinced.

The clutch of bars and restaurants which have now sprung up on both sides of the water are all new kids on the block compared to Aire Bar which continues to do precisely what Sparrow's Wharf always did – serve good food and beer in attractive and welcoming surroundings.

From the reclaimed, regenerated ancient thoroughfare of The Calls, you step down two flights of stairs into a bar of slate floors, industrial brickwork and dramatic arched ceilings; the architectural legacy of the time when these were warehouses and the busy Aire was the commercial lifeblood of the city.

One wall is dominated by a stylish long bar, which was doing three good Yorkshire ales when I last called in – Black Sheep from Masham, Yorkshire Blonde from Ossett Brewery and Leeds Best – as well as a good range of continental beers including Leffe and Hoegaarden.

If you've not been down here before, the flights of stairs lead you to feel you are heading down into some subterranean cavern, and the spectacular panoramic views can come as something of a surprise. At times the riverside deck sits just inches above the water, and it provides a great outdoor dining spot in summer, though during winter it's covered by a heated canopy making it possible to enjoy the changing Leeds skyline all year round.

Waterside Revival

Once seedy and dangerous, shunned and abandoned, the Leeds waterfront has found a new identity as a safe and attractive place to live, work and socialise.

The arrival of the twin attractions of Tetley Brewery Wharf in 1993 and the Royal Armouries in 1996 was the catalyst for major developments along both sides of the river, and though the former struggled and eventually closed, the latter remains a significant tourist attraction. It has been joined by bars, restaurants, offices, student accommodation and high-rise apartment blocks, in a rush to the waterside which has been echoed in many other British cities.

In Leeds, building has been so rapid and space at such a premium, that there is now an almost continuous string of both residential and commercial schemes along the whole length of the River Aire from Wellington Road in the west to South Accommodation Road in the east.

The Great Leeds Pub Crawl
Treasure Hunt

Make the connections to win £1,000!

Answered correctly, the clues overleaf point the way to a single answer – the name of a Leeds pub.

You have until 1 October 2012 to enter, with three great prizes up for grabs – £1,000 in cash, a pint of Leeds Brewery beer a day for a year, and a cocktail masterclass for five people at Mojo!

Each of the 18 clues below connects two pubs which are among the 35 featured on the five routes of the Great Leeds Pub Crawl – plus an extra pub which is now closed, but is also mentioned in the book.

And though some clues might seem to have several possible answers, and some pubs might seem to be the answer to several of the clues, no pub appears more than once among the answers.

By using your eyes, your mind and a little lateral thinking to make these key connections you will be ultimately led to another pub, which is the final answer to the treasure hunt.

The treasure hunt is not easy – it's not supposed to be. The internet may help you with some answers – but not all. Aside from some of the books which are mentioned in the bibliography, useful references I have used in assembling the treasure include a 1970s copy of the *AA Book of the Road* and *Leeds United: A Complete Record* (1990), but these are by no means crucial to working it out.

But whatever you do, and whichever pubs this trail leads you to – have fun, and enjoy a few good beers along the way!

www.greatleedspubcrawl.blogspot.com

Treasure Hunt Clues

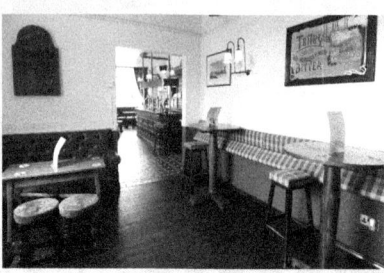

1) Connect here [right] to a pub where you can find a portrait of Ambrose Edmund Butler.

2) Connect a Royally-named pub with somewhere which became a Tetley pub on the day before Leeds United won 3–0 at Swansea.

3) Connect here [right] to a pub owned by an out-of-Leeds Yorkshire brewery.

4) Connect a pub which name-checks Barry Corbett and the Mustangs to a pub that is not the very top or top five, but it's there or thereabouts.

5) Connect a pub which has reproduced a famous Pennie Smith image to one which shares a name with the street it sits upon.

6) Connect a pub whose sign over the door is a celebrated antique, to one which has its own roll of honour – and no names on it.

7) Connect a Nicholson's pub to one with a stained glass picture of canal barges.

8) Connect a pub where the engraver Hawkins once worked, to one which is a letter from the seaside.

9) Connect here [right] to a pub where a tramcar's heading, possibly.

10) Connect a pub which could be worth over 75pts as a first move at Scrabble – to one where Corinne Bailey-Rae points the way to the gents.

11) Connect here [left] to a pub with a golden lion on the bar.

12) Connect a pub whose neighbour has 22 Victorian keystone heads, to somewhere that St Peter might feel at home.

13) Connect here [left] to a Leeds Brewery pub.

14) Connect two pubs, 300 metres apart, which would both score two at car cricket.

15) Connect here [left] to a place where a greyer bolthead could be made.

16) Connect one of the two pubs closest together with one whose name recalls an ancient profession.

17) Connect a pub where 1864 can be found in the stonework, with one due east from there.

18) Connect here [right] to a canalside watering hole.

Entry Form

Your name . . . .

Address . . . .

. . . .

. . . .

. . . .

Contact details

Tel: . . . .

Email: . . . .

The Treasure Hunt's ultimate destination:

. . . .

A brief description of how you came up with the answer.

. . . .

. . . .

. . . .

. . . .

. . . .

Your answer to the tie-break question: How many paces did it take the author to walk the full length of the Cross-City Ale Trail from the Palace to the Highland, passing the front door of each of the other five pubs en route?

. . . .

Post this entry form to:

Great Leeds Pub Crawl, Derby Books,
3 The Parker Centre, Mansfield Road, Derby, DE21 4SZ

Competition Rules

1. The competition closes on 1 October 2012.

2. The first prize of £1,000 will go to an entry which has successfully cracked the treasure hunt and correctly identified the pub which is the final solution. If there are more than one such correct entries, the tie-break question will then be used to determine the winner.

3. If no correct entry has been received by the closing date, the competition will then remain open.

4. All entrants must be 18 years old or over. Any person who is an employee or an immediate family member of an employee of Derby Books or any person directly connected with the competition is ineligible to participate.

5. The decision about the prizewinning entries and the distribution of the prizes will be made by the author and Derby Books, and will be final and binding. No correspondence will be entered into. Entrants submitting a stamped addressed envelope with their entry will be sent details of the solution and the winning entrants.

6. No responsibility will be taken by Derby Books or for any answers submitted that are illegible, misdirected, lost for technical or other reasons or received after the closing date.

7. The first prize will be a cheque for £1,000. The second prize – a pint of beer a day for a year – will be awarded in the form of tokens which may be redeemed at any pub in the Leeds Brewery chain. The third prize will enable the winner and four friends to enjoy a cocktail masterclass at Mojo. None of the prizes may be exchanged or transferred and no cash alternative will be offered. Only one prize will be awarded per entrant.

8. By entering the competition, entrants will be deemed to have read and understood these rules and agreed to be bound by them.

Pub Crawl Four

The Cradle of Industry

Holbeck was the birthplace of Leeds as an industrial powerhouse. It became in the late 18th century a hotbed of innovation, gaining for Leeds a new wealth and a new fame as a centre of cutting-edge engineering. Its confluence of waterways was as pivotal to the city's 18th-century expansion, as were the railways of the 19th century and the motorways 100 years after that.

This pub crawl celebrates a little of that, starting in the same pub which once slaked the thirst of those who laboured in Holbeck's factories and mills. It passes some of the splendid architecture which remains as a legacy of those times, revived for modern use. It also takes in some of the newer buildings which have sprung up south of the river in recent times, before crossing into the modern heart of the city to sample a few of the pubs close to the railway station.

Directions:

Start from the **Cross Keys** in Water Lane, turning right out of the front door to reach the **Midnight Bell**. Continue along Water Lane to turn right into David Street, and then left into Francis Place and on into Back Row where you will find the **Grove** at the far end. Beyond the pub lies busy Victoria Road, turn left here, and continue on towards the city centre into Neville Street. Turn left into the tunnels of Granary Wharf to reach the **Hop**, then retrace your steps to Neville Street, turning left again towards the city centre. The **Scarbrough** is directly opposite you as you emerge from the Dark Arches, and the **Prince of Wales** just across the road from there. To complete the journey, turn right out of the Prince into Mill Hill, right into Boar Lane and right into New Station Street where you'll find the **Brewery Tap** on your left.

Approximate total distance: 1 mile

The spectacular view of post-industrial Holbeck from the Sky Lounge of the Mint Hotel.

Detours:

Spectacular panoramic views make the **Sky Lounge** of the Mint Hotel in Wharf Approach well worth a visit. **Spencer's** is between The Scarbrough and the Prince, while at the opposite end of the railway station to the Brewery Tap, **JD Wetherspoon's** offers the kind of lively, keenly-priced drinking experience typical of the chain.

The Leeds-Liverpool Canal was once a crucial artery for the city's trade.

Cross Keys

Water Lane, LS11 5WD

0113 243 3711

www.the-crosskeys.com

The Cross Keys stands like a bulwark between the grim edge-of-town car parking of Globe Road and Water Lane, and the glitz, glass and post-Millennium confidence of resurgent Holbeck. With its striking exterior and attractive sunlit courtyard, it wouldn't look out of place on the Sussex coast. Step inside and you're transported still further south. There's something curiously French about it, a sort of shabby, careless, messy chic. The bric-a-brac and Victoriana might look like they were acquired at random from a boot sale, yet were no

doubt carefully selected for variety and their lack of connection to anything else in the place. Their eclectic nature is echoed by the pub's blackboards showing a rich choice of brandies, whiskies and artisan cheeses.

Huge beams criss-cross the central bar of a public house revived after years of pitiful decline. Red brick and mirrors, a lovely sweeping spiral staircase, a

panel fronted bar and painted plates each help create the homely feel of a lived-in yet cared for place, somewhere which might have been unchanged for centuries.

An atmospheric array of photographs up the stairs combines portraits of the famous, the obscure and the long dead. By contrast the toilets are more vibrantly decorated, the hunter green of the stately home giving way to a shocking crimson, like you are expected to perform your ablutions in some giant juicy raspberry.

There are four handpulls in all, and an appealing choice of foreign beers too. A menu boasting partridge, venison and rabbit marks this out as a true modern gastropub.

Out back the courtyard formed by new offices and flats makes a splendid summer sun trap. This brick and stone beer garden is a natural meeting place; the pub's community credentials underlined by quiz nights, farmers' markets and takeaway fish and chips, wrapped in newspaper.

History of Holbeck

Echoes of the city's industrial past are captured anew in the 21st century revival of Holbeck and its re-styling as an 'Urban Village'.

In the 18th and 19th centuries, Holbeck manufactured machinery, steam engines and cloth for export across the world, leaving behind a legacy of magnificent buildings. The splendid Temple Works reflects industrialist John Marshall's fascination with Egypt; the three towers of Thomas Harding's Tower Works honour classical Italian designs – the largest based on Florence's Giotto bell tower. Matthew Murray's Round Foundry, built in 1795, is reputedly the earliest surviving engineering works in the world.

Steam pioneer James Watt hired rooms at the Cross Keys from where his employees could spy on Murray, bribing his staff to reveal company secrets. Watt adopted many of Murray's innovative methods at his Midlands plant and

A work in progress: Thomas Harding's tower works – which once dominated the grim industrial skyline of south Leeds – are being revived for modern use.

Just as industrial Holbeck's finest buildings were inspired by Italy, so the modern Candle House apartment block echoes the Leaning Tower of Pisa.

tried to thwart his northern rival by challenging his patent applications and buying land in Holbeck to prevent the firm expanding.

Toward the end of the Victorian era, Holbeck's industrial prominence declined, the Cross Keys's gradual dereliction mirroring that of this whole area. The pub closed in the 1980s and by the time North Bar group found it, it was a tyre warehouse. A tasteful and comprehensive refit breathed new life into this empty shell, now transformed into a space as fitting for the office workers drawn here by Holbeck's revival as it was for the engineers and foundrymen of Murray's day.

Midnight Bell

Water Lane, Holbeck, LS11 5QN
0113 244 5044
www.midnightbell.co.uk

Above dramatic arches in Foundry Square, the paved patio behind the Midnight Bell, picked out in silver lettering are the words 'Welcome to Yorkshire'. Some 30 miles from the nearest county border, this is a statement of staggering confidence, as though you have never really reached the White Rose county until you've first set foot in Holbeck. A few years ago, this is the last place you would have come.

The rediscovery of this once-forsaken place as somewhere to live and work and do business is one of the signal success stories of Leeds over the past two decades. The attractive red brick Midnight Bell is as potent a symbol of this resurgence as the law firms, media groups and e-businesses which have flourished in a suburb which once tapped out the industrial heartbeat of Leeds.

The pub's name gives a clue to its ownership, Midnight Bell being the slightly sweet, rich, dark ale brewed by Leeds Brewery. This, their flagship pub, stands where once were the offices of Murray's foundry; cast iron plaques in the square – designed to rust and blend with the brickwork – tell his story.

Leeds products dominate on the bar of a pub which has been attractively and sensitively refurbished, rather in the style of a posh Lake District barn conversion. To the left of the door is an intimate, more subtly-lit area than the brighter, slightly livelier spaces around the bar. A staircase from beside the front door leads up to a dining room which is dominated by a brick fireplace topped by a huge stone lintel.

On the landing the plaster has been stripped away to reveal the lovely old red brickwork beneath and the ceiling pulled away to expose gnarled oak beams. The upstairs rooms lend themselves well to receptions, private parties and corporate events.

Drinking on the terrace at the Cuthbert Brodrick.

Outdoor drinking

The post-industrial rear courtyards of the **Midnight Bell** and the **Cross Keys** are among several much-loved outdoor drinking spaces in the city centre, precious square feet of fresh air and sky which gain a serious purchase on customers when the sun comes out.

The **Cuthbert Brodrick** is in Position A; its broad terrace essentially in sunshine from dawn until dusk, well on clear days anyhow. It offers a perfect vantage point across Millennium Square, whose new theatre, bars, live events and big screen sport have made this a focus of Leeds life since it was laid out a decade ago. The square's new **All Bar One** retains **Ha Ha's** big patio too, while the south-facing alleyway beside the **West Riding** in Wellington Street pulls in office staff at lunchtime and after work.

Other city-centre places to head to in the sunshine include **Aire Bar's** riverside terrace, the front and rear tables at the **Palace**, the tiny beer garden at the **Duck and Drake** with its amazing new age mural, the yards of **Whitelock's**, **The Ship** and the **Angel**, the rooftop terraces of the **Dry Dock** in Woodhouse Lane and Merrion Street's **Lounge**.

The Grove

Back Row Off Water Lane, LS11 5PL
0113 243 9254
www.thegroveinn.com

The Grove provides the most striking image of Holbeck's changing landscape. Built as a community local in the inter-war years, this traditional real-ale and music pub is surrounded by post-millennium glitz – offices, city living apartments and private car parks. It seems a miracle that the whitewashed brick Grove survived the concrete invasion, without being crushed beneath the sole of the boot-shaped Bridgewater Place.

To step inside is to take a small step back through time, to a public house oblivious to the change outside, where you can compare the relative merits of mild, bitter or stout while listening to a folk band or a guitar duo or just some drunk bashing out a tune on the piano.

The pub retains its attractive old tiled corridor entrance, a nest of rooms on both sides offering the kind of intimacy immediately lost in open-plan designs. Posters advertise the Grove's programme of gigs and concerts, which take place in the larger concert room to the rear. A piano and a tiny stage fill one corner of the room; bare floorboards, a big gilded mirror, a turned-wood hatstand and candelabra-style lighting lend the feel of some old west saloon. Here you drink off old sewing tables, whose wrought-iron treadles still rock in lovely satisfying fashion, turning the wheel which would once have driven needle through cloth.

Leeds Folk Club – which claims to be the longest-running group of its kind in the world – has been meeting here on Friday nights since the 1960s.

Only one room is served directly by a bar, but as at the Adelphi and the Garden Gate and one or two older pubs, the handpumps also front onto a corridor where hatches offer useful extra counter space. The Grove has always had a great reputation for its beer and the choice here is second to just about none. The range changes all the time, but you can generally reckon on Pendle and Daleside breweries being represented, while a mild, and a couple of interesting Belgians provide further distraction.

Despite the change all around and a confusing new configuration of roads

which make it slightly tricky to drive to, the Grove remains as relevant, as fascinating, and as worth visiting as it ever was. Perhaps more so.

Grove licensee Rachel Scordos and long-serving manager John Rowe.

Music pubs

On 27 October 1989, a little-known band called Nirvana played at the sweaty, dirty, much-loved **Duchess of York** in Vicar Lane. Others destined for international fame – including Oasis, Radiohead, the Manic Street Preachers – all graced the Duchess stage. Local acts like the Kaiser Chiefs, The Wedding Present, Chumbawamba and Corinne Bailey-Rae all cut their teeth here too.

The **Fforde Grene** on Roundhay Road was another launch pad for some big name bands, and the closure of these two legendary venues was a major blow to the live music scene, which is now concentrated in a clutch of smaller venues.

While some feature occasional or weekly live music, for others it remains a part of the daily diet, like at **The Well** in Chorley Lane and the **Pack Horse** in Woodhouse Lane.

Tribute acts can often be found at the **New Roscoe** in Bristol Street, itself a homage to the original Roscoe in Chapeltown Road, demolished to make way for the Sheepscar interchange. The Roscoe's terraced frontage is reconstructed in an almost life-size model beside the New Roscoe stage.

The Hop

Granary Wharf, LS1 4BR
0113 243 9854
www.thehopleeds.co.uk

Whoever chose to clad some of the sweeping groins of the Dark Arches in clean new brickwork should have first stepped inside the Hop to see how these beautiful industrial features could be better preserved.

The Hop is the first Leeds outpost for Ossett Brewery and is a perfect, tasteful re-use of this ancient space. Built into the sculptured brick of the Victorian water and rail terminus, the Hop is exemplary of the way a bar in one of the trendiest parts of town can co-exist happily with the past, embrace tradition and feel comfortable in its red brick skin.

Ossett products – Pale Gold, Silver King, Yorkshire Blonde and Excelsior – are lined up along the bar and further name-checked in sheets of etched glass whose contours follow the high curve of the archways. There are usually some

guest ales too, while blackboards list further choices – Erdinger Weiss, Belle Vue Kriek and Leffe Blonde among them the last time I called in. I can recommend the pies here too.

The occasional rumble in the brickwork and an accompanying ripple of the pint are a reminder that the arches still fulfil their original purpose, that of connecting Leeds to rail lines running north and east — to York and Hull, Newcastle and Edinburgh. The pub lies underneath the platform. Just west of here, a splendid viaduct and a derelict lifting tower are all that remain of the earlier Central Station, which closed in 1967.

The Hop's drinking space is enveloped and embraced by the architecture, its gaudy pop murals just as surely at one with the surroundings as the specially-commissioned stained glass. One wall features a stunning back-lit display of assorted beer bottles, while upstairs, where the brickwork fans out like the vaulting of some great gothic Abbey, there is a faint echo of the 1960s and the Cavern Club. It's up here that the Hop fulfils its second key function, as a fabulous live music venue.

The Hop's address is the Dark Arches, yet it also fronts onto a flagged and south-facing sunlit square, with views across to old buildings renascent as homes and restaurants and offices. A redundant lock gate and a dammed stretch of canal are centrepieces of the square, the once-practical preserved as the aesthetic and as a reminder of the purpose these structures once served.

The Dark Arches

Almost 150 years old, the Dark Arches span the Leeds-Liverpool Canal, and were built as part of an expansion of the railways, allowing city station to be established on its present site, high above a right angled kink in the River Aire. No less an authority than Pevsner's Architectural Guide describes this mysterious, mighty brick cavern as 'one of the grandest sights of the city today'.

The rediscovery of the Dark Arches and Granary Wharf as a centre of business and as a place to live is a model of city regeneration; a fine new use of a space once abandoned, yet now adapted for a much-changed world. Once packed with barges and boats, this was a smoky, dirty, noisy hub of trade which teemed with life at the heart of a city whose lifeblood was the trade in coal and cloth, wool and grain.

To wander through the arches now, to see and hear the rush of the weir, to smell the water and to wonder at this feat of visionary engineering and construction is to take a little glimpse back to a Victorian city on the up.

Scarbrough Hotel

Bishopsgate Street, LS1 5DY

0113 243 4590

www.nicholsonspubs.co.uk

Driving into Leeds from the M1, the Scarbrough, with its hanging baskets, green and gold tiling and the legend 'Ind Coope's Burton Ales', always makes for a welcome sight as you emerge from the dark arches.

The pub name is often mis-spelled with an additional 'o', but it is actually named after Henry Scarbrough, the first licensee here in 1823, rather than the Yorkshire resort. It stands on the site of a moated medieval manor house, Castyll Hall, though the present-day pub is an extension of an 18th-century rebuilding.

In the 1890s it was owned by Fred Wood, who also owned Leeds City Varieties; winning acts from the pub's talent contests were soon transferred across town to the theatre's stage.

Scarbrough licensee Toby Flint checks out the quality of the beer.

There are numerous competing theories as to why it's more commonly known as the Scarbrough Taps – or even the Scabby Taps – from it once being owned by the waterworks, to tap dancers auditioning here in Wood's time. No-one seems sure.

The interior is essentially a large L-shape, wrapped around a long bar topped with a great range of real ale handpumps. It's big and comfortable, and shares the high standards of food and drink of its stablemates the Palace and the Victoria – and attracts a lively crowd.

Just as at the nearby Prince of Wales, the Scarbrough makes the most of its south-facing pavement to create a narrow outdoor drinking space, which is a big draw when the sun shines, despite the relentless traffic on the inner-city loop.

In long-serving licensee Toby Flint, The Scarbrough has one of the real characters of the local licensed trade, and he regularly organises beer festivals in the pub, putting in an extra temporary bar and serving upwards of 50 different beers over the course of a few days, often in conjunction with the nearby Grove.

Leeds Beer Festival

Held every spring, Leeds CAMRA Beer, Cider and Perry Festival is one of the biggest in the UK, and a popular fixture on the city calendar, attracting huge crowds to Pudsey Civic Hall.

The event is themed – past examples include the seaside and all things Celtic – with beers chosen from right across the UK to fit the theme, often very loosely. Some brewers create ales especially named for the event, or at least rename existing ones to ensure their place on the festival's long bars.

In addition to the dizzying array of real ales, there's always music, good food and a weird and wonderful choice of ciders and perries, while the global beer bar offers further cosmopolitan choice.

The Prince of Wales

Mill Hill, LS1 5DQ
0113 245 2434

Despite a chequered history that has seen it closed and re-opened several times, the Prince of Wales clings to life. Back in business, this oft-overlooked city-centre gem is looking good and doing well.

Always a little in the shadow of the Scarbrough Taps, its short black frontage might be easily missed, or simply bypassed by those familiar with its rather down-beat reputation from ages past. But a smart refurbishment and a good choice of real ales has made this place well worth checking out.

Perhaps more than any other Leeds pub, the Prince of Wales has the feel of one of those lovely old taverns which you can sometimes stumble across in the backstreets of central London. Even so, Yorkshire beers dominate here — the

The changing colours of the Prince — red in 1998, black in 2003, white in 2008.

three handpumps were dispensing Copper Dragon and Leeds Brewery products on my most recent visit.

The decor is all shades of coffee and cream, with an attractive wood-panelled bar in one corner of the wedge-shaped front room, which has been fitted with a plush black foliage-patterned carpet. This motif is echoed in the upholstery of the comfy long banquettes, with their high leather backs.

A quieter, smaller and more intimate room to the rear is a little more basic of decor and furnishing, with bare wooden floors. In both rooms, old black and white prints of city scenes and great old Leeds buildings can be found around the walls.

A small rear yard and a huddle of pavement tables offer some surprising outdoor drinking space, the former a remarkable suntrap just a stone's throw from the Dark Arches.

Great lost pubs

The Prince survives, but with pub closures running at something like one every eight hours nationally in 2008–09, it was inevitable that some Leeds favourites would be lost. And while each is mourned by its regulars – great locals like the **Shoulder of Mutton** at Potternewton, the **Blooming Rose** in Beeston, the **Skinner's Arms** in Sheepscar, the **Hark to Rover** in West Park – others represent a yet greater loss to the city's heritage.

The Cock and Bottle, a famous old coaching inn from the early 1700s, was incorporated into the Schofields Headrow store in 1938 and finally demolished in 1961.

The late-Victorian **Rising Sun** on Kirkstall Road, with its mosaics and glasswork and curving oak bar, is irreplaceable. Renamed the Trading Post, its windows are stacked with bric-a-brac. You could weep, if only at the irony of a period-piece pub being churned into a down-market antique shop.

The **City of Mabgate** in Burmantofts was a fine alehouse, steeped in city history; the majestic old **White Stag** in North Street – now demolished – was architecturally a poor man's Garden Gate, and a true Irish pub from the time when Leeds was host to a huge Irish community.

Few suffered the same fate as the splendid old **Florence Nightingale** opposite St James's Hospital, which was destroyed in a gas explosion in April 2008 – much to the chagrin of doctors, nurses and hospital visitors, for whom this was a welcome and appropriately-named bolthole.

Brewery Tap

New Station Street, LS1 5DL

0113 243 4414

www.brewerytapleeds.co.uk

This is not only Leeds Brewery's official 'tap', it is also an offshoot of their whole brewing operation. From the upstairs bar, windows reveal the gleaming stainless steel of the pub's own micro-brewing operation which produces their full-bodied Leodis pilsner and a changing selection of small-volume cask ales.

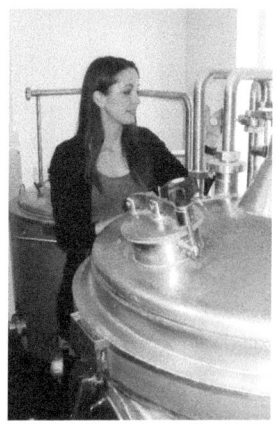

Manager Nicci Cassidy in the Brewery Tap's on-site microbrewery.

The Brewery Tap holds a prime location on the approach to Leeds City station and is a welcome watering hole for those arriving in the city or preparing for departure. Behind its frosted glass frontage is a comfortable drinking space alongside a long central bar which features the familiar trio of Leeds ales, plus a changing choice of appealing alternatives – including hard-to-find Tetley Cask Mild when I last popped in.

There's always a good range of continental beers too, a point underlined by a display of enamelled advertisements for the likes of Vedett, Liefman's and wonderful Budweiser Budvar. A beer society meets here regularly to taste and discuss selections from the Brewery Tap's cosmopolitan fridges.

There's a relatively small choice of food on the menu. It's chiefly steaks, burgers and salads; but attractive presentation, sizeable portions and gastropub values speak of a confident bar, doing its own thing and doing it all rather well.

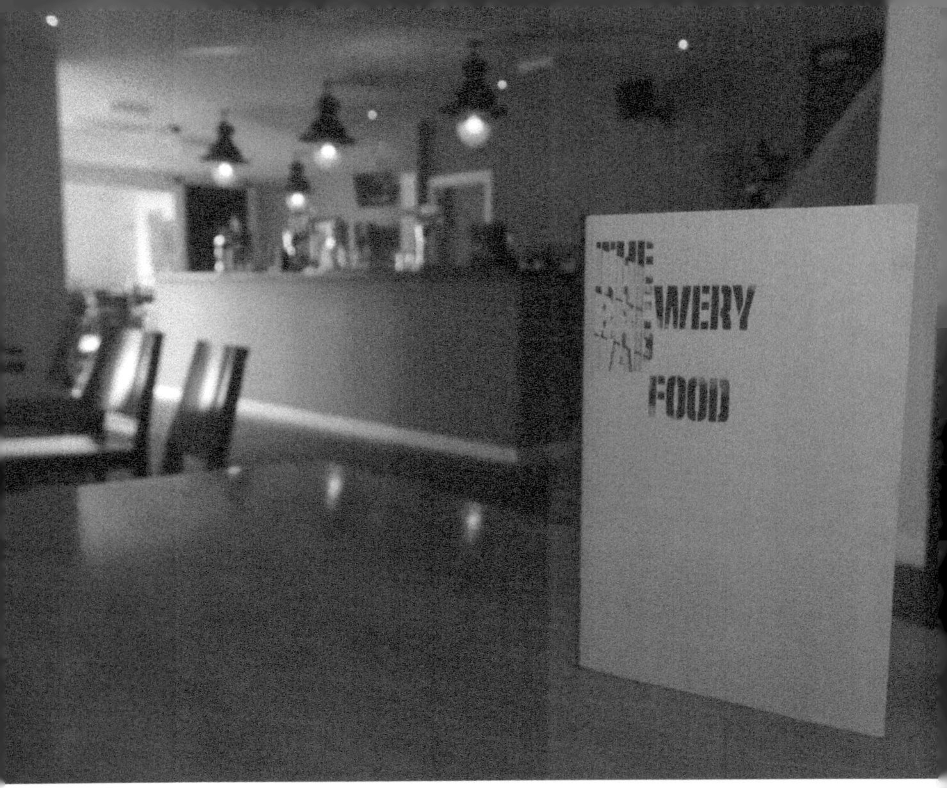
WERY
FOOD

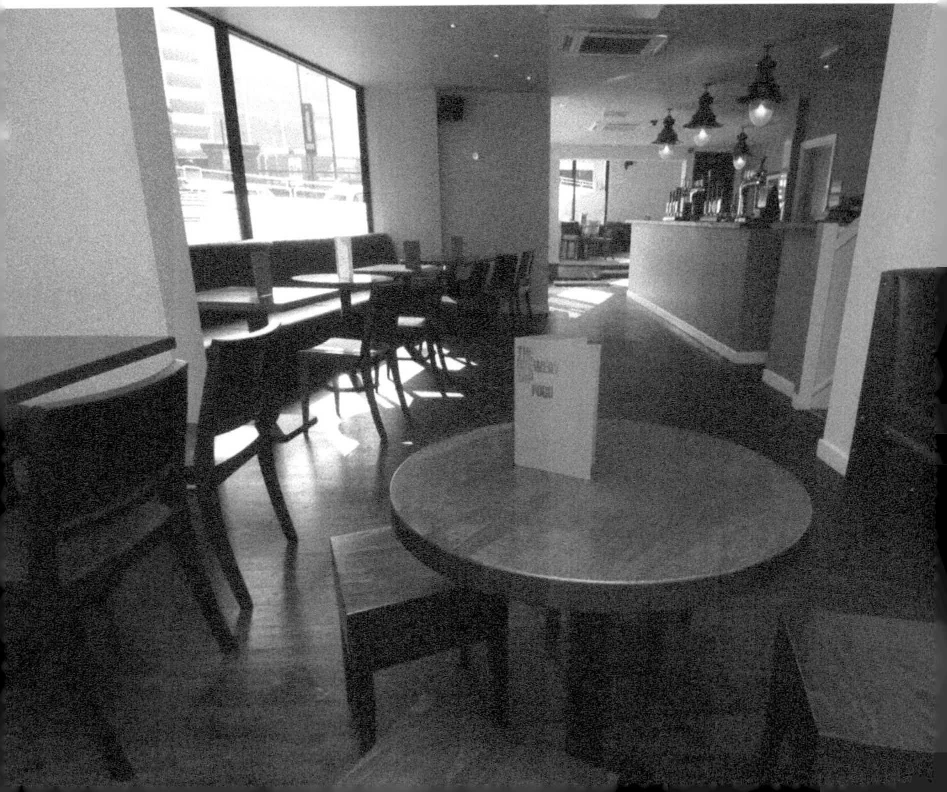

Leeds Brewery

Now that Tetley's has gone, Leeds Brewery is in prime position to occupy their traditional marketplace. They have the name, they have the momentum, they have a clutch of great bars – and more importantly they have a range of three main beers which have already gained significant purchase on the public consciousness in their target city market.

Partners Michael Brothwell and Sam Moss both studied history at York – but developed a love for real ale on the Minster city's thriving circuit. Michael had a spell learning the ropes at York Brewery, before they headed west to establish their own brewery, hidden away down a Holbeck back street.

Its success was almost immediate. By late 2007, just a few months on from their first mash, Leeds Brewery products were being eagerly drunk in the Prince of Wales, the Scarbrough Taps, the Grove, the Vic and the Palace – right in Tetley's back yard.

The brewery's pump clips, with their distinctive curvy tear-shaped rhombus shape, are now a welcome sight on bars across the county, while their four pubs – the **Brewery Tap, Pin, The Midnight Bell** and the **Garden Gate** are each distinctive and each worth visiting.

By naming its flagship brands Leeds Best – a firm and full bodied bitter – and Leeds Pale – zesty and refreshing – the company has stolen into territory which Carlsberg carelessly overlooked. Their Midnight Bell is richer, darker, fruitier; the super-strength Gyle 479 a soporific soup of rich caramel and toffee and black treacle, vanilla and chocolate.

Sam Moss of Leeds Brewery.

Pub Crawl Five

A Trip Around The Suburbs

At something like 15 miles, this circuit needs either a dedicated driver, a substantial taxi kitty or an encyclopaedic knowledge of city bus routes.

As much as I have suggested it as a pub crawl, it should also serve to offer a flavour of some of the many and varied suburban pubs which can be found dotted around the city. Each serves its local community well but is also worthy of a trip across town to visit.

There are plenty more, of course – the Red Lion at Shadwell, the Broadway at Beeston, the Station at Cross Gates, the Commercial at Churwell, the Bay Horse and Myrtle at Meanwood, the Tut and Shire at Yeadon and the Gaping Goose at Garforth were all close contenders for inclusion.

Directions

From the **Beech**, head into the city on Tong Road and the A58(M) inner ring road, leaving on the A58 towards Meanwood. Turn left at Sheepscar following Meanwood Road and left into Cross Chancellor Street and on into Melville Road for the **Chemic**. Turn back, and left into Meanwood Road and after a mile right into Stainbeck Road. Follow this to its end, crossing Scott Hall Road, then turning right into Harrogate Road, and park alongside the main road in Chapel Allerton for the short walk along Regent Street to the **Regent**. Continue to the Stainbeck Lane junction, turning right and following this to Stainbeck Road, turning left, and continuing into Grove Lane, before turning right on Otley Road where you find **Woodies** after a half a mile. Turn back towards Headingley and right at North Lane, continuing into Kirkstall Lane. At the Kirkstall crossroads, turn left into Kirkstall Road, where the **Cardigan** is about another mile, on your left. Then it's back to the crossroads, left at Bridge Road, following signs for Bradford. After a mile and a half turn right into Rodley Lane, for the **Rodley Barge**. From here continue to the A6120 Leeds Ring Road, turning right. Stay on here until you turn left just after Horsforth Hall Park. Park in the car park here, crossing the road to walk a short way up Town Street for the **Town Street Tavern**. **Approximate total distance: 15 miles.**

Detours:

The number of other pubs you could visit on this tour is only limited by your capacity for alcohol, the depth of your pockets and the patience of your designated driver. But the route takes you close enough to Kirkstall for you to sample the **Old Bridge** and the  **West End House**; while your drive from Chapel Allerton to the Otley Road offers the twin delights of **Alfred** and **East of Arcadia** at Meanwood and the sublime **Beer Ritz** off licence on Weetwood Lane. It's also worth making the short detour to Weetwood Hall Hotel, where you'll find the beautiful stone-built real ale paradise of the **Stables**, possibly my favourite hotel bar anywhere.

Beech

Tong Road, LS12 1HX
0113 263 8659

The famous name of Melbourne Ales is picked out in a yellow and black mosaic in the pub's green-tiled frontage. With its tiled floors, basic working fireplace and shapely leather banquettes, this 1930s alehouse has plenty to recommend it.

When CAMRA published their book of *Yorkshire's Real Heritage Pubs* early in 2011, the Beech was trumpeted as the last substantial survivor of the inter-war expansion of the Melbourne empire, when Pontefract architects Garside and Pennington built around a dozen pubs for the city brewery. An illustration showed how the sumptuous terracotta of the tiles and ceiling matched the polished wood of the curving bar front and a row of leather stools.

When I visited shortly before this book went to press, I found it much changed, the walls stripped bare of pictures and no real ales on the bar, despite a proud line of Tetley handpumps. Leeds United crests, painted into the ceilings and external doors, are a more recent addition to the decor and symptomatic

of a pub which has been allowed to go into decline, despite its listed building status. It is under new management apparently, so hopefully things will begin to improve.

Virtually next door, where Tong Road and Wellington Road meet, another old Melbourne pub, the Crown, sits alone, abandoned and unloved, its slightly grander ivory and green tiled facade now scarred with hardboard panels erected to keep the squatters out and posters advertising local events. There seems little hope of a revival here.

Long gone – The Fox Inn at Woodhouse.

Melbourne Brewery

It's more than 50 years since Melbourne Brewery was subsumed into the Tetley's empire, yet at the **Beech**, the **Crown**, the **Templar**, the **Palace**, the **Manor House** and the **Royal** in Bradford, and a fair few other pubs around West Yorkshire, there are plenty of reminders of that famous old name.

The mosaic at the Beech is a rarity, but in several others the Melbourne Ales name remains in block letters above the door, the company's logo of a red-and-gold cloaked bowing courtier still visible in the original windows.

Melbourne, based in Regent Street, was originally the Leeds and Wakefield Breweries Company. It is perhaps credit to Tetley that, once these pubs changed hands in the 1960s, they didn't set about erasing the name of their former rival. Perhaps they had better things to do.

Chemic Tavern

Johnston Street, LS6 2NG

0113 245 7670

This two-roomed alehouse has served the good people of Woodhouse for generations. And under the stewardship of sisters Dawn and Ruth Edwards it has survived where a number of other locals have gone to the wall.

Both the splendid Beer Engine free house and the archaically named Swan With Two Necks have been redeveloped for housing, though the frontage of each has been at least partly preserved in the new look, as at the much-missed City of Mabgate, close to the city centre. More recently the Bricklayers Arms – which once boasted of serving the finest ploughman's lunch in Leeds – has also shut its doors. Its long-term future is in doubt.

Sisters Dawn and Ruth Edwards at the Chemic.

The Chemic stands a little way back from the main road in an elevated position which might suggest an air of superiority over its surroundings. With its imposing stone frontage, authoritative gold lettering and pub sign of Victorian scientists conducting an experiment, it might even seem a little aloof and forbidding.

Yet nothing could be further from the truth. This is a pub which stands absolutely at the centre of Woodhouse life, the focus for events and music as well as being the day-to-day meeting place for this inner-city community. The famous Arkwright's fish and chip shop, another pillar of the community, is right next door.

A short flight of steps leads into an entrance lobby; the main bar is to your left, the taproom a little further on. The former is long and welcoming and comfortable, with two real ale handpumps and a host of lager fonts competing for attention on the short bar.

The rather threadbare carpet reflects the pub's relentless footfall, though the upholstery on the long banquettes is holding up well. Mirrors and sepia prints of local scenes hang around the walls.

Beside the bar a window looks through to the rear taproom, smaller and more spartan with bare floorboards, a dart board and a tiny stage from where live acts entertain. And while some pubs have a piano, here there's a double bass propped up in one corner, just waiting to be played. A sizeable pile of board games offers some quieter recreation.

Ridgeside Brewery

Down the road from from the Chemic, in a charmless inner city industrial unit in Sheepscar, using equipment salvaged from a jam factory, Leeds's second newest brewery is starting to make its presence felt. Brewer

Simon Bolderson of Ridgeside.

Simon Bolderson built the whole system himself combining his long experience of home brewing with the opportunity afforded by redundancy to turn his passion into a business. He moved his home brew kit into onto the site as well, using it as a test bed for his recipes, and a little over a year on from his first brew, Ridgeside has begun to make a name for itself – not least at the excellent East of Arcadia up the road in Meanwood, which always seems to have one of its beers on the bar.

There's quite a range from the well balanced Ridgeside Challenge session beer, to the rich and dark Black Night, by way of their easy drinking Pale and the beautifully soporific Southern Cross.

I say 'second newest' with good reason. As this book was in preparation, news came that Dave Sanders of Elland Brewery was busy reviving brewing in Kirkstall. Given his track record, we can surely expect big things of the new Kirkstall Brewery Dissolution IPA is already a personal favourite, and top prize for its Black Band Porter at Keighley Beer Festival is surely the first of a host of plaudits to be heading that way.

The Regent

Regent Street, Chapel Allerton, LS7 4PE
0113 2939395

This perennial suburban favourite has continued to do
the simple things well, while the Chapel Allerton drinking circuit has exploded
and expanded in ways quite unimaginable to those who lived there 20 years ago.

The Regent is a Tetley's house and its two-room, nooks-and-crannies layout
is largely unchanged since it was built in the early nineteenth century. At that
time it would have stood alongside the main Leeds-Harrogate turnpike road, as
did the older Nags Head nearby, though by the middle of the 19th century, the
road layout had shifted to its present pattern, with the main Harrogate Road
some fifty yards west of the pub's front door.

There's always a good choice of real ales here, often Tetleys and Deuchars and an interesting selection of alternatives, while Sky Sports TV and a suntrap side beer garden help to pull in the punters. Its twin front doors open onto either lounge or taproom – this is a pub where drinkers often have their favourite side, and stick to it religiously. In winter, open fires make this a cosy refuge from the cold.

And as the Queen's has been churned into a Toby Carvery, the Mustard Pot has shifted markedly up market, and the Nags has become a little less salubrious, the Regent has remained true to its roots, and can confidently claim to be the best genuine and unspoiled pub in the village.

It really comes into its own during the Chapel Allerton Arts Festival, in late August and early September, when Regent Street is closed to traffic, and the live music stage erected just yards from the pub's front door. The bar does a roaring trade, the beer garden is in a prime position for those who want to soak up the sun, the music and the carnival atmosphere.

The Mustard Pot.

Chapel Allerton Circuit

The development of Chapel Allerton as a trendy suburb, a desirable postcode, and as a night-time destination, is one of the more remarkable changes which Leeds has experienced in the past two decades. And though there had long been a clutch of pubs they have now been joined by a bewildering, and seemingly ever-changing selection of bars and restaurants.

Those keen to bar-hop can enjoy a lively circuit starting at the **Queen's** on Harrogate Road, recently re-styled as a Toby Carvery, before nipping into **Further North** and then Regent Street for the **Regent** and down Hawthorn Road for the **Nag's Head**.

From here head back to the Stainbeck Lane junction and enjoy a little tour around **Hub, Zed**, the **Mustard Pot**, the **Suburban Style Bar** and **Angel's Share**. On warm summer evenings, customers spill out onto the pavement patios of each of these, lending a continental feel to a suburb which has utterly reinvented itself.

Further down Harrogate Road is the splendid **Seven Arts**, which does good food and hand-pulled ale – plus an eclectic range of music, drama, film and comedy in its intimate rear theatre space. Another quarter mile ends our tour at the **Three Hulats**, which does everything you would expect of a Wetherspoon's pub.

Woodies Alehouse

Otley Road, LS16 5JG
0113 278 4393

Woodies is one of those rare pubs which has managed to maintain a serious student following without alienating its locals. Its location, a mile or so beyond the bedsit heartland of Headingley and Hyde Park, means that it couldn't simply survive on student trade alone. Ever since its days as the Woodman, this has always been a pub which has managed to attract a good mixture of customers, from the young lads who gather around the pool table, to the businessmen and office workers who stop in for a pint on the way home and to the pensioners who come in for the good-value food.

It also perhaps helps that the Otley Run starts – rather than ends – here, when the participants are lively but sober, unlike when they arrive at venues closer to town.

What they all come for is the beer – and this place has long had a reputation for serving quality real ale. Yet despite the name 'Alehouse', and the varied array of pump clips along the bar, this is no freehouse, and in fact a part of the expansive Greene King, which has bought up pubs as hungrily as it has rival brewers.

So wander in here, or any of its stablemate pubs like The Roundhay at Oakwood or the New Inn in Headingley, and you might find the octagonal motoring badge of Old Speckled Hen, the oval rural scene of Ruddles County and the crusader's shield of Olde Trip. Once regional marques of their own, these are all now part of the GK empire.

Woodies has always thrived as a popular venue for live televised sport. The proximity of Headingley stadium, as well as the sports facilities at Weetwood, Glen Road and Becketts Park have made this a watering hole of choice for those to whom sport is an essential part of life, either as spectator or participant. Its numerous high-definition screens make this the ideal place to take in the big game.

The Skyrack and Original Oak stand opposite each other in central Headingley. Their names recall the ancient 'Scir Ac' – or Shire Oak – under which meetings were held in medieval times. The Oak finally collapsed during a gale in 1941.

The Otley Run

Woodies is the starting point of the city's most infamous pub crawl. On almost every day of the week, groups in fancy dress attempt this marathon drinking session, which takes in every pub along the Otley Road – and a few just off it – between Far Headingley and the city centre.

The accepted route is **Woodies, Three Horseshoes, New Inn, Arcadia** (no fancy dress allowed), **Headingley Taps, Arc, Box, Skyrack, Original Oak, Hyde Park, Library, Pack Horse, Eldon, Fenton, Dry Dock**. It's quite a long walk – the stretches either side of the Hyde Park are occasionally done by bus – and the better-organised groups have a designated timekeeper to keep drinkers to schedule.

Few students at the city's three Universities manage to reach the end of their studies without attempting at least one Otley run, for some it is a termly ritual.

For many of the city's sixth formers, it has become the standard rite-of-passage on turning 18. It can get very messy.

The author, front, and friends Scott, Jon and Tom in full Otley Run mode.

Cardigan

Kirkstall Road, LS4 2HQ
0113 274 2000

The original Cardigan Arms has its origins in the 18th century, but 100 years later had become so run down and disreputable that the magistrates only renewed its license on learning of new owner Benjamin Greaves's plans to redevelop the site.

The modern-day Cardigan is very much how Greaves will have remembered it. He employed Leeds architect Thomas Winn to draw up plans for the new building, which opened in 1895. Winn was also responsible for the design of the

Adelphi and the nearby Rising Sun, which closed in 2009, though its splendid Victorian frontage survives.

Winn's plans are displayed in one of the four intimate drinking spaces which open off from the Cardigan's central bar. With its commercial room and smoke room, billiard room and snug, the Cardigan was a place of relaxation, refreshment and entertainment. The old outbuildings include a disused brewhouse.

Plush upholstered banquettes maximise the seating space; tiled fireplaces, wooden panelling and bell pushes to summon table service each tell of a gentler time.

Etched glass, stained glass and leaded glass speak of an era when new pubs were decorous, elegant, comfortable — and a little home from home. For many of its customers no doubt these were more opulent surroundings than the ones they would find at home. It's a Grade II listed building, but then so is the Rising Sun.

The Charge of the Light Brigade

The name Cardigan is inextricably linked with the events of 25 October 1854 when the Seventh Earl of Cardigan led the ill-fated Charge of the Light Brigade at the Battle of Balaclava during the Crimean War.

By 1854, the original pub had already stood here for 50 years, taking its name from the local landowners, the Earls of Cardigan – family name Brudenell.

The Seventh Earl had enjoyed a chequered career both as an army officer and politician during which time he displayed both incompetence and generosity to roughly equal degrees, though the miscommunication at Balaclava was the fault of others higher up the chain of command.

On being ordered to lead the charge he did so with the resigned cry: 'Here goes the last of the Brudenells,' charging headlong down the 'Valley of Death' into the teeth of the Russian guns. More than 100 died, yet remarkably, Cardigan survived.

His family name and title are preserved both in the pub name and a clutch of nearby streets; his act of bravery at following seemingly suicidal orders is remembered in a collection of paintings in the front room of the pub.

Dressed as the Seventh Earl of Cardigan, licensee Trevor Ives joined wife Joyce to celebrate the pub being granted Heritage Status by Joshua Tetley in 1986. Trevor, who died in 2002, was a much-loved landlord at the Cardigan for 18 years.

Rodley Barge

Town Street, Rodley, LS13 1HP
0113 2574606
www.therodleybarge.co.uk

Long lines of pump clips on the beamed ceilings of the Rodley Barge tell of a community local with a commitment to giving its regulars an ever-changing choice. It is rightly proud of its Cask Marque accreditation – displaying the handpump logo of this highly-regarded scheme which serves as an independent guarantor of real ale quality.

The Barge sits alongside the Leeds-Liverpool canal at Rodley, perhaps 250 metres south of where the waterway is crossed by the Leeds ring road at Calverley Bridge. The canal and the River Aire take separate winding courses west from here, but converge at Rodley, where a clutch of factories – now closed – traded on their proximity to these twin arteries of commerce.

The rediscovery of the canal as a place of recreation has given the Barge a fresh constituency among the walkers, families and cyclists who use the waterside as a place to spend their leisure time.

Its roadside beer garden is south-facing, making this a significant draw in the summer; to the rear, a narrow terrace offers customers the chance to drink beside the water. Solid lunchtime pub grub is another good reason to make the trip out this way.

Staff, families and regulars from The Owl and The Rodley Barge come together every year to create Rodley Beer and Music Festival.

The Owl

Directly opposite the Rodley Barge is the Owl, another real ale community pub which is on the up, under the loving stewardship of part-Pole, part-Glaswegian Gina Howard and her family.

Gina worked in a bank for years, and supplemented her income as a barmaid at the excellent Abbey in Horsforth, well known as a real ale and live music venue. It is this same formula which has revitalised the Owl. Yorkshire beers dominate on the bar, though the selection changes regularly.

The two pubs come together every summer to run the Rodley Beer and Music Festival, an event which has grown in both size and significance, helping to nurture the community spirit of a suburb which has a new-found confidence. The event runs for four days over the August Bank Holiday weekend, for two of them the road is closed to traffic.

Town Street Tavern

Town Street, Horsforth, LS18 4RJ

0113 281 9996

www.markettowntaverns.co.uk

To enter one of the 15 pubs in the Market Town Taverns chain is rather like visiting one of those distressed-wood alehouses you sometimes find as life-size displays in folk museums.

Although each quite different, all bear some of this confident, expansive company's hallmarks. The curving black-on-gold capital script is one, as are the enamelled advertising panels and framed archive posters of beers of the world. Each of these mark out the Town Street Tavern as a member of this popular and successful chain.

This was once a butcher's shop and then an off-licence before being given the MTT treatment. And while there are these recognisable themes, this is no manufactured 'look' in the way that some of the bigger pub chains might set about it. Each of the Market Town Taverns has its own character, rather than some cheerless design imposed to meet the company's corporate image.

Here, pump clips and beer mats around the walls show off the various real ales, predominantly from Yorkshire breweries, which have been on sale here in the past. A short walk across the laminate flooring from the front door brings you to a bar where plenty more vie for your attention on the counter. And if eight real ales are not enough to whet your appetite, then how about a range of continental beers which includes the likes of Leffe, Warsteiner, Erdinger and a fruit beer?

The decor is very simple – cream walls above sage green panelling, the furniture fairly spartan wooden chairs, stools and benches. The strategic use of etched glass screens discreetly divides the main room into two, while a narrow beer garden to the side provides some welcome outdoor drinking space.

Bar meals are available here at lunchtimes, but – in common with a couple of the other MTT joints – the food menu broadens in the evenings when an upstairs restaurant offers a full bistro-style menu. It's child and dog-friendly too.

Market Town Taverns

As pub chains go, they don't come much better than Market Town Taverns. The Knaresborough-based group is behind some of the best born-again alehouses in Yorkshire. Places like the **Bar T'At** in Ilkley, **Muse** in Wetherby, the **Narrow Boat** in Skipton and the **Old Bell** in Harrogate.

And while each of those have been a significant addition to the local scene, MTT has also managed to gain a reputation for making a success out of venues where previous occupants have seemingly struggled. Its premises in Great George Street had been the Portland, the Hogshead and twice been the Waterhole, before being characteristically revived as **Veritas**.

Its excellent **East of Arcadia** stands on the site of the old Beckett's, which was allowed to slide from slow failure into dereliction. East is now as potent a symbol of Meanwood's renaissance as the giant Waitrose superstore across the road.

Picture credits

The vast majority of photographs in the Great Leeds Pub Crawl appear by courtesy of Yorkshire Post Newspapers – with special thanks to Paul Napier, Andy Manning and Keith Hampshire. The Refectory music images (page 54) were by Dave Siviour (left) and Steve Riding (centre and right), and appear by courtesy of the University of Leeds. The images of the Town Hall Tavern (pages 63–64) and of pub food (page 80) are courtesy of Chocolate PR; pictures of Mojo (pages 85–87) and Oporto (interior) are by courtesy of Sharon Brigden of SLBPR. Pictures on pages 23 (bottom), 24 (top and second top), 31, 32, 33, 40, 41, 42 top, 67, 71, 72, 73, 159 top, 160, 161, 167, 168–69, 170, 173 and 174–75 are by Mark Bickerdike. Those on pages 26, 27, 28 (top), 29, 37, 42 (bottom), 48, 49, 50, 51 (top), 52, 53, 55, 56, 83 (top), 88, 90, 91, 92, 105, 116 (bottom), 121, 125, 131, 137, 138 (top), 144, 147, 163, 164, 165 are by the author. The picture on page 176 appears with the kind permission of Mrs Joyce Ives. The picture on page 171 (bottom) was taken by a very drunken Ben Jenkins, dressed as Buddy Holly, on his 18th birthday pub crawl.

Bibliography and further reading

To a greater or lesser degree, each of these books has assisted my preparation
of the Great Leeds Pub Crawl – and in my gradual understanding of pubs, of
beers, of the great British pub culture – and of local history:

Yorkshire's Real Heritage Pubs edited by David Gamston (CAMRA Books)

Fifty Great Pub Crawls by Barrie Pepper (CAMRA Books)

Old Inns and Pubs of Leeds by Barrie Pepper (Alewords)

Real Ale in Central Leeds edited by Adrian Rankin (CAMRA Books)

The Leeds Pub Trail Compendium edited by Mark Firth (CAMRA Books)

300 Beers To Try Before You Die by Roger Protz (CAMRA Books)

Chapel Allerton – from village to suburb by R Faulkner (Chapel Allerton Residents
Association)

The Knights Templar in Yorkshire by Diane Holloway and Trish Colton (The History
Press)

Twenty First Century Leeds – Geographies of a Regional City, edited by Rachael
Unsworth and John Stillwell (Leeds University Press)

Leeds – Pevsner Architectural Guide by Susan Wrathmell (Yale University Press)

Leeds Old and New by Percy Robinson (Richard Jackson Limited)

Far Headingley, Weetwood and West Park by David Hall (Far Headingley Village
Society)

Historic Otley Ale Trail by Phil Greaves and Greg Mulholland (Otley Pub Club)

Index

BV - #0089 - 280426 - C0 - 210/136/12 - PB - 9781780912349 - Gloss Lamination